TRISH WYATT

DON'T REPORT RAPE

Find Out Why This is The Advice From a Survivor of an Extremely Violent and Life-Threatening Sexual Assault and Rape in 2018, in Regional Queensland Australia

First published by Ultimate World Publishing 2022
Copyright © 2022 Trish Wyatt

ISBN

Paperback: 978-1-922828-81-1
Ebook: 978-1-922828-82-8

Trish Wyatt has asserted her rights under the Copyright, Designs and Patents Act 1988 to be identified as the author of this work. The information in this book is based on the author's experiences and opinions. The publisher specifically disclaims responsibility for any adverse consequences which may result from use of the information contained herein. Permission to use information has been sought by the author. Any breaches will be rectified in further editions of the book.

All rights reserved. No part of this publication may be reproduced, stored in or introduced into a retrieval system, or transmitted in any form, or by any means (electronic, mechanical, photocopying, recording or otherwise) without the prior written permission of the author. Any person who does any unauthorised act in relation to this publication may be liable to criminal prosecution and civil claims for damages. Enquiries should be made through the publisher.

Cover design: Ultimate World Publishing
Layout and typesetting: Ultimate World Publishing
Editor: Vanessa McKay
Cover image copyright license: Serg Zastavkin-Shutterstock.com

Ultimate World Publishing
Diamond Creek,
Victoria Australia 3089
www.writeabook.com.au

WARNING WARNING WARNING

I have written this book from my heart with as much detail as possible. As easy as it would have been to leave a lot of the gory and embarrassing details out, I truly feel it is important that people understand exactly what sexual violence is, to understand this issue accurately in today's world.

Content Warning

Please be advised that the contents of this book reveal intimate personal details about my experience as a survivor of an extremely violent sexual assault and rape. Themes mentioned in this book include sexual violence, rape, sexual acts, date rape, consent, suicide, mental health, pornography, drugs and alcohol use. Understandably, this can be very difficult to read and should only be read by mature audiences.

Language Warning

I am considered to have a bit of a potty mouth, whilst there isn't a lot of swearing, there are a few 'f' bombs.

Don't Report Rape

Trigger Warning

If you do decide to read-on, please keep these warnings in mind and if you are triggered, please reach out for support. These issues are rampant in our society, yet barely discussed.

If you decide not to read-on or feel unable to read-on, please know I fully understand and respect your decision.

LIFELINE AUSTRALIA

www.lifeline.org.au

Phone 13 11 14 available 24 hours / 7 days - Australia's largest crisis support line. Anyone in Australia can speak to a trained Crisis Supporter over the phone, any time of the day or night.

Lifeline Text 0477 13 11 14 available 24 hours / 7 days - Australia's first SMS-based crisis support service, any person in Australia can receive support from a Crisis Supporter by text message, any time of the day or night.

Online chat available 24 hours / 7 days - The online chat service is available for people who prefer to type than talk. Any person in Australia can chat with a Crisis Supporter through the Lifeline Australia website, any time of the day or night.

1800RESPECT

www.1800respect.org.au/violence-and-abuse/sexual-assault-and-violence

Sexual violence can be a form of domestic and family violence; if you or someone you know has experienced sexual violence, you can contact **1800RESPECT** on **1800 737 732** or through the website.

Dedication

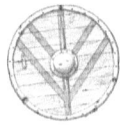

This book is dedicated to every single woman and girl who has been a victim of sexual violence.

The women who are not yet able to talk about their experience.
The women who have carried their trauma for years and never told a soul.
The women who, for whatever reason were unable to report the crime to police.
The women who blame themselves.
The women who took their own life waiting for a trial.
The women who did report only to be further traumatised by our reporting and justice system.
The women who did report, only to see the offender found not guilty due to our outdated and unjust laws.

I see you, I believe you and this is for you.

Disclaimer

The purpose of this book is to educate our community and law makers on what it is actually like for a woman, in Australia, to go through sexual assault trauma and its aftermath.

I have shared my experiences to highlight the systemic injustices in our legal system and the desperate need for an overhaul of laws in the area of sexual crime.

I want to make it abundantly clear to you, as the reader, that the offender in my case was found NOT GUILTY on ALL charges, by jury trial in Queensland District Court.

I have recalled the details with honesty and integrity. I have endeavoured to make this book as factually accurate as possible.

I have written this book with the assistance of my police statement, court transcripts, journal entries, emails, text messages and my memory.

It is for both legal and moral reasons that I have changed names and identifying factors of persons mentioned within this book, to ensure their privacy is respected.

This is my experience, my perspective, my story and my opinion...... no one else's.

Contents

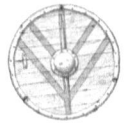

Introduction	1
Chapter 1: The Morning After	5
Chapter 2: My History	13
Chapter 3: Reporting the Crimes	25
Chapter 4: Giving my Statement	33
Chapter 5: The Arrest	43
Chapter 6: The Assault	51
Chapter 7: 2018 First Year Waiting for Trial	59
Chapter 8: 2019 Second Year Waiting for Trial	71
Chapter 9: 2020 Third year waiting for trial	81
Chapter 10: 2021 Trial Prep	101
Chapter 11: Trial Day One: Morning Session	109
Chapter 12: Trial Day One: Afternoon Session	121
Chapter 13: Trial Day Two: Morning Session	131
Chapter 14: Trial Day Two: Afternoon Session	141
Chapter 15: Trial Day Three	149
Chapter 16: The Verdict	163
Chapter 17: Where to from here?	177
Appendix 1: Trauma Response referencing	183
About the Author	185
Speaker Bio	187
Acknowledgements	189
Disclaimer	191

Introduction

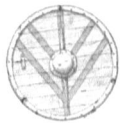

In January 2018, I was violently raped and assaulted over an eight-hour period after meeting up with someone I met on a dating site. This book will take you through the journey of how a woman who had been married for twenty years navigates this new world of online dating and details the intimate horrors that occurred during the assault. I will link my experience to well-documented and researched responses to trauma and explore the meaning of the term – sexual violence.

I will share with you the confronting experience of how I survived that night, followed by comprehending the horrors of what happened. Next, we will discuss the process I went through when deciding to report these crimes to Queensland Police Service (QPS) followed by the traumatic three-and-a-half-year wait, with my life in limbo, trying to heal and just get on with my life while waiting for a trial.

You will see, right from the moment I tried to report the crimes (the very next day) the hurdles, the red tape, the barriers I faced and fought through in an attempt to hold a violent sex offender accountable. I think it's fair to say the general public realise that going to court for these types of crimes is hard for survivors but it so much worse than just hard, it's fucking horrific, and society should be outraged.

While reading this book, you will be shocked, horrified, saddened, outraged, and angry. Possibly even in disbelief that our so-called justice system is so flawed and so broken that it provides a legal loophole or a get out of jail free card for rapists.

I want to build national attention on the issue of sexual violence and consent particularly advocating the immediate removal of the 'mistake of fact' defence which allows rapists to escape prosecution and the introduction of an affirmative consent model.

I hope that this book will spark a deep desire within you to stand with me and speak out about this topic. Nothing we have done as a society has worked. So far, nothing is changing. We have been trying to address violence against women in society for decades, why are we still fighting for this and why haven't significant changes been made? What will it take for authorities to listen to us? Women are taking their own life waiting for a trial, in my darkest days I pondered it myself and for what? A three-percent conviction rate, it's just not worth it.

I want this book talked about on every radio station and every television show possible, until my story is heard; because it's not just my story, it's the story of every survivor as well as those who didn't survive.

My thirteen-year-old daughter talked to me about the title of the book yesterday and wondered if I may be sending the wrong

Introduction

message, I told her that if she told me she was raped today, I would not allow her to prosecute. I would take her to the police station and let them know who did it and what happened but that would be it. We would walk out of the police station and focus on healing. I would refuse to let her be subjected to such a cruel and barbaric system designed to protect the offender while shaming, blaming and traumatising survivors.

Despite the horrors of my assault and experience with the justice system, it is not all doom and gloom. You will discover a hidden gem within this story, with the formation of a tribe of women - My Tribe, a collection of diverse women, a sisterhood who supported me through this. Women who believed me, encouraged me, and continually reminded me that I was doing the right thing, that I had done nothing wrong and that absolutely none of this was my fault. These women gave me strength and hope when I didn't feel I could go on. These women, along with my family and partner, are the heroes of this story.

Chapter 1

The Morning After

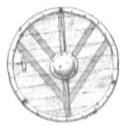

Saturday January 12th, 2018.

I am in a motel room. I am dazed and confused, pacing in a small circle, not knowing what to do. The sun was rising, lighting the dimly lit room, a man lay naked in the bed. I see used condoms scattered over the floor. I feel panicked. My mind is telling me to grab my bag and get to my car, but my body isn't so sure and continues pacing.

I remember the horrific details from the night before and I start wondering; *what if I wake him up, what if he sees me leaving and gets angry, if I just leave without saying anything he might know something is up*. He knows my car and where I live. I was frightened of his reaction; I couldn't let him think anything was wrong. I stick with my survival plan. I pretend nothing is wrong, everything is fine.

Don't Report Rape

My body is sore. My chest feels crushed, and I can barely touch or move my neck without it hurting. My mind is foggy and I feel dirty. I take a shower, the warm clean water runs over my battered body. The water stings my torn genitals.

I get myself dressed and grab my bag. *OK, let's go!* I tell myself but again my body isn't so sure. I find myself pacing again. Trying to keep appearances as normal as possible, I walk around to his side of the bed, lean down give him a quick kiss and say,

'I have to go.'

I step back quickly in case he grabbed me and headed for the door. I was out! I ran down three flights of stairs. Got in my car. Locked the doors and drove home.

Now, I know my behaviour here is very unusual, I can hear you saying: Why would you do that? Why wouldn't you just leave? Why did you have a shower? Why didn't you just leave as soon as you could? These are questions I have asked myself over and over. Questions I have worked through many times with my therapist. Questions I was grilled about while on the stand during the trial. I had just experienced over eight hours of repeated sexual violence and rape where I truly believed I was going to die. From what I know about trauma from my career in social services and now with my own personal experience, I can tell you confidently the answer to these questions is because my behaviour was a classic and very normal trauma response.

I am sure most people have heard about the fight, flight and freeze trauma responses, well there is a fourth one, not so well known called fawn. Scholars first started using the term fight or flight in 1915. Since then, numerous theories have emerged. The most recognised are Fight, Flight, Freeze and Fawn also known as the 4F's of trauma; a term coined by therapist and trauma expert Pete Walker.

Below is a brief summary of each:

Fight – An act of active self-preservation where you react with anger and aggression. This can look like yelling, physically fighting and throwing things.

Flight – Avoidant behaviour when we feel we can escape the threat. A knee jerk reaction run, to go and go now, running away, heading for an exit and an overwhelming need to leave and the ability to attempt to do so.

Active responses like fight/flight can put us in more danger as any attempt to run or fight brings more attention to us.

Freeze – A protective strategy that can be anything from playing dead, going numb to disassociation. When the trauma event is so horrific, you can't escape and it's just too much to bear. A person can detach from their physical body, their surroundings, body sensations and feelings. It can be like they are watching the traumatic event unfold in a movie or viewing the event from above or outside of their body. Freezing is the bodies attempt at becoming non-threatening to the perpetrator.

In rape situations we will choose what will assure our survival. The more life threatening the situation, the more likely we will go to the bottom of the hierarchy of freeze.

Fawning – A behavioural response that comes out of the fear and freeze responses. A strategy used to keep the perpetrator on side, not wanting to say or do anything to upset the perpetrator in an attempt to minimise the abuse and to stay alive. This can look like complying, people pleasing, going along with, and submitting to what the abuser wants. A common response during rape, the need for it to just hurry up and be over with. It is a common scene played out in movies and TV shows when someone is assaulted, or their life is threatened.

Most of the time in overwhelming/traumatic situations we enter into a mixed physiological state. This can feel really confusing when we have fight/flight/freeze/fawn all expressing themselves at once, it will make us do things like wander around the room in an attempt for the nervous system to figure out what to do.

It's important to note that these stress responses are involuntary, which means it is not a conscious choice, it's a survival instinct that we all have as human beings. Evolutionary wise these responses have served us well, allowing us to escape or survive life threatening situations. They also provide a simple framework to explain and understand human behaviour with regards to how we respond or behave during these types of situations. Furthermore, it is the perfect defence for any type of victim blaming when explaining why a victim behaved a certain way.

In a criminal trial that involves extreme sexual violence over an eight-hour period experienced by the victim as a life-threatening situation... wouldn't you assume that a trauma expert would be called as a witness to explain this basic human response to a jury? I expected this as standard practice and was horrified that the Department of Public Prosecutions (DPP) had not done this for my case and in fact stated to me directly that she has never heard of that being done. I literally felt my mouth drop open when she said this, I looked over to Lesley my support person, friend and fellow social worker and she had the same look of horror on her face. I found this out the morning of court, literally just before taking the stand. I was absolutely horrified and devastated. This highlights my first recommendation.

Recommendation 1 – All trials MUST have a trauma expert as a witness

All sexually violent cases must have a trauma expert as a witness for the trial to educate the jury on trauma responses and stop blaming the victim for how she responded.

We have to stop victim blaming and this is the only way in which this can be done. Additionally it would allow for the free flow of information and education so the jury could understand a basic human response to trauma. I can hear you saying, surely they don't victim blame in court? Yes, they can, and they do. In my experience victim blaming appeared to be standard practice in our criminal courts in sexually violent crimes. The victim is judged on how she responds to the event; she didn't scream or run away etc. Remember the 4F's of trauma? Which explain why victims respond in certain ways. It is not a conscious decision, it is a very common and normal trauma response. But the jury isn't educated on this….. why?…… why is this information being withheld from the jury?

Disturbingly in my case, multiple examples of this are obvious and, in my opinion, unjust, outdated and just plain cruel as discussed further in Chapter 11, The Trial. I was victim-blamed, slut-shamed, fat-shamed and career-blamed (if that's even a thing). As a society, I thought we had moved past - what were you wearing? You could have left couldn't you? And so on.

Don't Report Rape

How can we as a society publicly push a message to stop victim blaming when our courts don't even acknowledge it and withhold information from the jury explaining the basic psychology of a trauma response.

Below is a poem my thirteen-year-old daughter Violet authored as part of an English task to write a poem about an important issue:

But what was she wearing... right?

Hands roaming her body
Her mouth taped shut
Afraid to speak up
because …. What was she wearing, right?

Fear drowning her body
her legs paralysed
wondering if this would be her last day alive
but… She could have said no, right?

His arms around her neck
as she fights against his hands in a hurry
while her vision starts to go blurry
but….. Maybe if she hadn't provoked him in that skirt… right?

She feels uncomfortable looking in the mirror
trying to erase the memories with a shower
feeling gross in her own skin
but… Maybe if she fought harder, she could have stopped him... right?

Written by
Violet
August 2022, age 13

The Morning After

How can she, a child, have such an understanding of this and our law makers don't?

Arriving home after the assault.
Thankfully my children were with their dad for the weekend. My mum was staying with me at the time and as I walked into the house it was clear she didn't approve of me staying out all night even as a forty-three-year-old woman; she said to me,

'What kind of a mother goes out all night?'

I didn't respond and went straight to bed and spent most of the day there.

I was still so confused and tried to process the events of the night before while being constantly reminded of my sore and tender body. I try to normalise the experience, a classic coping strategy for dealing with trauma. It's simple, if I tell myself it was a normal consensual sexual encounter, I don't have to face the reality of the horrific life threatening situation I was in. These were the kind of things I was telling myself: *I did meet for consensual sex, alcohol and cannabis were involved, I didn't scream, I didn't leave, maybe the violence I experienced is considered normal sexual behaviour by today's dating standards …. it had been over 20 years since I was last on the dating scene.*

Trying to process, trying to make sense of what happened, was extremely confusing, confronting, and overwhelming. Physically and mentally, I was absolutely exhausted and just needed to sleep and slept excessively.

Chapter 2

My History

I grew up in a family of five in south-west suburban Sydney; both my mum and dad worked full-time jobs. I am the youngest of three children. My sister is four years older than me and my brother is two years older than me. I guess I consider my upbringing normal, for an average middle-income family. I have great memories of camping with extended family and friends during Christmas and Easter school holidays. Riding bikes and playing out in the street with neighbourhood kids, a standard eighties childhood really.

I always felt like the peacemaker in my family. I hated conflict and arguing, and I often felt like I was sorting out arguments between my siblings. Their personalities just clashed, and they often argued particularly as teens. Reflecting on this I can see my natural tendency is to fawn; it's what I did when my parents argued, which scared me as a child, or when my siblings fought. I

Don't Report Rape

just wanted the uncomfortableness of how I felt during those times to be over. A classic example of this was when my sister threw a bottle of tomato sauce across the room at my brother (back then tomato sauce bottles were glass), it missed him, smashed against the wall, and looked like a crime scene. They both stormed off, mum and dad were at work, so there is Trish with the dustpan and cloth cleaning the walls and floor, getting things back to normal.

I was a carefree and vibrant fourteen-year-old girl in grade eight at an all-girl catholic school when I first experienced the evil in this world. A neighbourhood friend and her older brother were having a party at their house as their parents were going away. I arranged to stay the night, of course my parents didn't know their parents were not home. It was the first time I had lied about where I was going, my first time breaking the rules so to speak. It was at this party I drank alcohol for the first time, it was at this party that I had my first sexual experience, it was at this party that my virginity was stolen, it was at this party I was raped.

My History

Up until now, I had only ever told one friend and my first husband about this assault. I have carried so much shame and blame for so many years, I owe it to my fourteen-year-old self to acknowledge it, release it and use it to fuel my fight for justice.

At the party, I remember not feeling well, most likely from my childlike body trying to process the alcohol I had drank. I never felt unsafe, I had no reason to think I was unsafe, the world as I knew it was a pretty good place. I went into an empty bedroom closed the door, turned off the light and laid down on the bed hoping to sleep it off and feel better. I must have fallen asleep as I didn't hear anyone enter the room. But someone did enter the room. I woke up to a sixteen-year-old boy laying on top of me, penetrating me, he was forcibly holding both of my wrists above my head so I couldn't move. I recognised this boy; he is a friend of my friend's older brother. I had never spoken to him, but I knew who he was, he was known in our neighbourhood. I lay there wanting him to just hurry up and get it over with, there was no talking, no conversation, he finished and left the room without saying a word. This was the first time I experienced freezing and leaving my body, but I didn't put the pieces together until I was learning about disassociation at university fifteen years later.

At the time, I didn't feel I could fight or flee, my automated response to this trauma was to freeze and disassociate. I remember leaving my body and watching the scene from above like I was watching a movie. At some point I re-entered my body, got up and went to the bathroom. There was a small amount of blood when I wiped myself, so I folded up some toilet paper and put it in my underwear.

At the time, I only ever told one person: my dear friend Hayley. Hayley and I were best friends at school, and we also worked together in the toy department at Kmart. The day after the assault at the party, Hayley and I had a shift at work together and it was here while tidying the toys on the shelf that I told Hayley what happened the night before. We were both in shock and disgusted trying to make sense of it and then in the distance, I see the teenage rapist, the boy from last night with his friend walking through Kmart, looking all cheerful and confident. *What the fuck? Why is he here?* I panic and hide (flight response).

Hayley went and spoke to them. Turned out he assumed we hooked up the night before when he raped me and actually believed that we were going to date now. I was so angry, how fucking dare he do what he did and then think I would date him now? What the actual fuck I was so confused. Hayley told him I wasn't interested, and they left the store. I thank God to this day that I never saw him again. I pretended it never happened, I never told anyone except Hayley; not my mum, not my sister, not a teacher, not my doctor, not an aunty, no one. I dealt with this alone, pretended it never happened and I got on with my life.

I have fond memories of my teen years, there were about ten of us girls in our group at school, who remain friends now. I guess I was considered a risk taker and probably more promiscuous than the other girls which contributed to the shame and negative self-image I felt internally. Turns out victims of childhood sexual abuse often demonstrate promiscuous behaviour in their teen years, something else I didn't know at the time. Externally I was confident, carefree, and funny. I went through to grade twelve, had a part time job, played sports, went to parties on weekends and had a few boyfriends. I graduated year twelve in 1995 and worked in various office roles.

I met my first husband in 1996 and we married in 1999 when I was just twenty-one years old and he was twenty-two, certainly

My History

considered young at the time. We were married seven years before we had the first of our four children.

The next major event I navigated was in 2013 and led to my change in profession. My mum was struggling with severe depression. In her darkest days, my mum was suicidal, required electric shock treatment and admission into a mental health facility. Seeing my mum so unwell was hard, I have always been very sensitive to other people's energy and it's easy for me to feel what others feel which I now know is my ability to empathise with others, however, at the time I was getting stuck in my mum's depression, I felt helpless and didn't know how to process any of it.

I saw a flyer for a workshop for family members of someone with a mental illness which I decided to attend. While attending this workshop I learnt so many great coping skills and was educated on mental illness, I was super impressed and wondered why everyday society didn't know this stuff. I quizzed the facilitator on what qualification she had and soon after I enrolled full time into university. I graduated with distinction, a bachelor's degree in Applied Social Science, proudly the first in my family to obtain a tertiary education. I felt proud and confident, that I had found my passion, my purpose was to help others.

I started my career in Kings Cross Sydney at The Wayside Chapel, a homeless drop-in centre where I worked with some of the most vulnerable members of our community for example sex workers, addicts, trauma, victims of abuse, neglect and mental health struggles. Often referred to as the outcasts of society, the type of people the general public like to think don't exist in our country. A dear friend I met at university, Lesley (who was my support in court) also worked here, it was a truly amazing experience both professionally and personally.

Don't Report Rape

From the hustle and bustle of Sydney, we moved to Roma Queensland. Our little family of four (our six and four year old daughters) headed to the outback. Roma offered work opportunities for my husband whose brother and his family also lived there. Roma is approximately a five-hour drive inland from the Sunshine Coast and boy was it a culture shock. I worked in foster care in Roma with some great mentors and would travel to more remote towns to support foster carers in St George, Injune, Mitchell, Surat, and Dirranbandi. I witnessed the additional and unique struggles families living in rural and remote communities faced. I really loved our time there and I made some wonderful lifelong friends. One of them being the extremely funny and lovable, Yoie (short for Yolande), a midwife and true country girl who delivered our third daughter, Piper at the Roma Hospital.

After about two years we moved to our dream home in regional Queensland. It was absolutely perfect, a beautiful high set Queenslander home on twenty acres, two horses, chickens, a few cows, so close to the beach that you could hear the waves, beautiful tropical gardens, a tennis court, dirt bike track and a massive shed to allow my husband to work from home. Our main reason for moving was so my husband could work from home and not have to work away. I have always worked full time and been the primary carer of our children. For most of our married life my husband worked away, often two to three weeks at a time with one week home, ultimately, I believe this is what started the deterioration of our marriage.

My first job here was in the Flood Recovery Program which supported people impacted by the 2013 floods which devastated the community. I then moved into Intensive Family Support where I supported families experiencing abuse and neglect, families whose children were at risk of being removed by child safety. Families who

My History

were heavily impacted by domestic violence, substance abuse, mental health and often their own childhood trauma. This work was tough and confronting but also rewarding and desperately needed in our community. This is the role I had when I went on maternity leave when I had our fourth child.

While halfway through my maternity leave, in June 2017, I decided to leave my husband of twenty years. Many things led to me leaving, it was the hardest thing I have ever had to do but also something I knew I had to do. It was the right thing to do. Our marriage was unhealthy not only for us but also our children and I did not believe anything would change. I know and acknowledge the pain this caused my husband and children. I saw it in their eyes and felt it in my heart, but something deep inside told me I had to do it. I left the family home with my four children in tow: aged twelve, ten, five and six months. I had never rented before and had no rental history, and I was not working as I was on maternity leave so finding somewhere to live was tough. We spent a short time in my sister's granny flat before moving into what we called the 'Yellow Beach House'. It was tiny, filthy and rundown but it was right opposite the beach, and it was ours.

When I left my marriage, I initially had no interest in dating however after a few months I did start thinking about it and I decided to investigate internet dating and see what it was all about. This was really daunting, I hadn't been single since I was a teenager, over 20 years ago and boy oh boy how the dating scene has changed. I mean we didn't even have mobile phones when I last dated, we met face to face in pubs, clubs, and nightclubs. Excited and nervous I dived into this new world and I signed up to a dating site called Plenty of Fish, (POF). I created a profile and uploaded some nice photos and before I knew it messages started coming in. I have to say, it was exciting and fun chatting with different people, flirting, and ultimately working out who you might want to date. Apart from the man who assaulted me, I had been having good experiences with the type of men I was chatting with.

It was apparent that sending dick pics was a standard practice that I found hilarious, like seriously? I was often asked for nudes, which I never sent, not that there is anything wrong with that if that is what you do, it just wasn't my thing. When I did meet someone in person, they were often shocked that I looked exactly like my photos. I thought that was so strange, I mean if you plan to meet someone you need to look like your picture, right? Once you match with someone you chat over messenger through the app and if things progress, you swap mobile numbers and go from there. This is how I met my perpetrator. I was due to return to work on Monday 14th January 2018. I matched with my perpetrator late December 2017 when he messaged me on 22nd December. I replied to his message on 4th January 2018, we exchanged messages through the POF app and went from there. After swapping mobile numbers he asked for some pics, here is the dialogue:

My History

Trish-   I have heaps on POF and sent two more photos of myself.

Perpetrator-   I meant ones that ya wouldn't send to anyone else

Trish-   Nup, lol

Perpetrator-   So what do you like to do?

Trish-   live music, beach, adventure, star gazing and trying new things

Perpetrator-   I like going to the beach with my son and making music and expanding my conscious awareness.

Trish-   Oh I love that, I'm right into energy healing, natural therapies, spiritual awakening etc

(Yep, got me hook line and sinker as they say)

Perpetrator-   Oh really

Trish-   Really! I also make orgonite (resin, crystals and metal) pyramids and pendants. Check out my fb page Orgonite Magick.

Perpetrator-   OK, cool, will do

Perpetrator-   So what's for dinner?

Trish-   Dinner at my sisters place tonight, BBQ for my niece's birthday. How about you?

You get the idea, general chit chat, getting to know each other.

We agree to meet Friday night 11th January. My last weekend before returning to fulltime work after maternity leave.

Perpetrator-   OK, your place or mine

Don't Report Rape

Trish- Can't do mine, my mum is staying with me. How about a Pub to start?

Perpetrator- Is she living there? How about a motel room on the beach?

OK, so yes this does raise a red flag for me, I wonder if he is married and that could be why he is avoiding meeting in public.

Trish- Staying with me while she tries to sell her house in Sydney. Your definitely single right?

Perpetrator- Yeah are you?

Trish- Yes definitely

Perpetrator- Cool so you want to just get a motel as we both have our mum's staying with us?

Trish- lol, ah OK

Perpetrator- You don't believe I'm single?

Trish- Yeah I do, Just wanted to check. First meet up I prefer a public place for safety reasons.

Perpetrator- Yeah I might murder ya :P , Motel is a public place :P

Trish- lol you might!

If I only knew what I know now ...

Perpetrator- I will be making you scream but it won't be from getting murdered

Trish- Big call ....

Perpetrator- Big something anyway

Trish- Really..... you're a bit naughty..

My History

Perpetrator- Sorry :P

Perpetrator- OK so motel room tomorrow night?

Trish- I am only free tonight

Perpetrator- OK will see how I go getting a good room

Trish- OK

Perpetrator- Still waiting for my sexy pic ?

Trish- Not gonna happen...

Perpetrator- (winking emoji)

Perpetrator- So I'm booking a motel room for tonight?

Trish- Yep

He then phoned me, we spoke and laughed. He suggested I grab something to eat on my way, I did find this strange, I guess I just assumed we would go downstairs to the pub to eat. He was 10 years younger than me, and I found him physically attractive from the pictures I had seen. He had olive skin, dark hair, physically fit looking body, some tattoos, and his dating profile said he was six foot. Height is a bit of a thing for me as I am quite tall (5'9). He seemed very quick witted and funny. I really loved the fact that he said he was into raising his spiritual consciousness as that was something I was into too, and I was yet to meet a man who had that same interest.

I was feeling excited but nervous and looking forward to the evening ahead. I dressed as I would for any first date (given I had only been on two first dates since leaving my marriage, so I'm really, really nervous about the whole thing) a nice floral knee length dress, hair curled, and makeup done. I wasn't sure I would stay the night, but I put a change of clothes in my bag just in case.

Don't Report Rape

4:48 p.m.   Perpetrator- On my way now

4:49 p.m.   Trish-   OK, I'll be leaving shortly

On my way, I dropped into my local bottle shop and saw a good friend Justine who was working there at the time. Justine commented on how lovely I looked, asked what perfume I was wearing and asked about the date I was heading to. I showed her some pictures of the man I was about to meet, she told me to be safe and have a good time. I purchased two bottles of pink Moscato and a four pack of rum and coke. I'm so excited, playing my favourite tunes and singing along in the car.

5:39 p.m.   Perpetrator- OK, I just got here. Top floor at the end. Room 301

5:40 p.m.   Trish-   OK I am about 15mins away

5:50 p.m.   Perpetrator- No worries

6:00 p.m.

I pull into the motel carpark and turn off my car, music stops. As I sit in the driver's seat, in silence, something or someone is telling me not to get out of the car, *don't get out of the car Trish*, something deep inside me…. *Don't get out of the car Trish*. It did sound like a warning *and certainly got my attention… however, I said things to myself like it will be fine, your being paranoid, he is spiritual, he has to be a good person, right?*

I could feel my heart beating, I took some deep breaths to calm my nerves and I got out of the car. I made my way upstairs to the motel room, top floor, end of the row, room 301.

Chapter 3

Reporting the Crimes

Sunday, 13th January

After sleeping to escape most of Saturday and Saturday night, on Sunday I met with a friend down the beach, and we talked about Friday night. It was this friend who really put into perspective what had actually happened, and she said to me, you have to report, you have been raped Trish, you need to report. I really didn't want to hear this, I didn't want to report, I didn't want to deal with this, I just wanted to get on with my life; just like my fourteen-year-old self did all those years ago.

But I wasn't fourteen anymore, I wasn't a shame filled naïve teenager, I was a grown ass woman, a professional woman, a woman who fights for justice, a woman who deals with the devastating effects of violence every day at work and most importantly, I was a mother. It was this connection that eventually led me to report. My friend said to me these six words - 'imagine if it was your daughter'. That was it, I knew I had to file a report, I couldn't not and as much as I didn't want to, I knew I had to. I owed it to my fourteen-year-old self to do it differently this time, to do what's right, to report to authorities and hold the perpetrator accountable and to protect potential future victims.

Keep in mind that it's Sunday 13th January and I was expected to return to my full-time job the next day.

Midday Sunday I went to the local Police station with my friend. I approached the front desk, the person at the counter asked me how she could help me. Nervously I told her I'd like to speak with an officer about a rape, she asked us to wait while she called someone. A young officer opened the door to a small interview room and called us in. Still in a lot of denial and confusion, I remember saying things like, *'I am not even sure if a crime had been committed,'* the officer asked for some details of what took place and said to me that it was rape and that from what he heard multiple crimes had been committed.

I said, 'okay, then what do I need to do now?'

The officer wasn't sure, he left the small room and asked his sergeant. He came back and proceeded to tell me how hard the reporting process is for victims, that it's a long and difficult process and that I should really go home and think about reporting. I told him I was going ahead with reporting, and he ducked out of the room again to speak with his sergeant and when he returned, he said you really need to be sure about your decision because if I take your statement now and spend hours writing it up and you decide not to report, then it would have wasted all that time. The young male officer handed me a business card sized brochure on strangulation which highlighted the seriousness of this type of injury and how to treat it.

Shocked by the response and not wanting to put anyone out, I left the police station with my little brochure to think about if, in fact I was going to report. Knowing I had full intentions to come back and report the next day, I asked what I needed to do if I wanted to go ahead with reporting and he advised me just to present back at the station. It was disappointing how many times the young officer had to leave the room to check with his sergeant on how to proceed with this type of crime.

Monday, 14th of January

I emailed my team leader and my manager advising them what had occurred and that I wouldn't be returning to work as expected. I received nothing but empathy, support and strength from these two women and the organisation I was working for at the time.

10 am
With my friend for support, I anxiously return to the police station ready to divulge the intimate and gory details of the assault. Same process, speak to reception, sit and wait, get called by an officer from the interview room to come in. Another young officer calls us in where I proceed to tell him that I would like to go ahead and report a violent rape and assault. He has a puzzled look on his face and told me I need to get a medical done first. The officer told me that my doctor/general practitioner (GP) or the hospital can do the medical and even recommended I go to my GP as it would be more comfortable with someone I know. While sitting in the interview room I called my doctor's office and was able to

get an appointment with my regular GP at 2:45 p.m. The friend I was with and only person I had told, had other commitments, and could not hang around for my appointment so I continued the process from here on my own.

2:45 p.m. Monday 14th January
I attended my GP's office for my 2:45 appointment as advised by the officer earlier the same day. When I saw my GP, I broke down and told her the details of the assault on Friday night and that I needed a medical examination as I wanted to proceed with charges.

I was visibly distressed and sobbing when recalling the details. My doctor told me that she is unable to conduct the examination as she is not qualified. She stated that this type of examination is arranged through Queensland Police Service (QPS). I told her it was a constable from the local police station that told me I could have it conducted by my GP. The constable then checked with the acting Senior Sargent who confirmed that yes, your GP can do the medical. With a look of disbelief and horror on her face she apologised profusely and told me that information was incorrect, she told me there are specially trained forensic staff at the hospital that conduct these types of examinations. I am appalled that the information given to me on such a serious crime, by a police officer and confirmed by a sergeant, was completely incorrect. Now it appears I have wasted most of my time today running into dead ends.

Feeling confused and defeated and knowing now that I would have to present at the phone and window of the local Hospital emergency dept, raised my anxiety levels through the roof. Can you imagine standing in emergency and explaining to the triage nurse through a glass window, on a phone, in front of the entire waiting room? It would be so much easier to just go home and forget about reporting all together, but I couldn't. Instead, I asked my doctor to write a letter explaining the situation so I could just hand it to the nurse at the emergency department and not have to speak through the glass and have the people sitting in the emergency waiting room hear this very personal information. My doctor offered follow up care, handed me the letter and I nervously headed to the emergency department on my own.

3:30 p.m. Monday 14th January
I presented at the emergency department, and hand my letter through the glass window, I was asked to sit in the waiting room and wait for the triage nurse to call my name.

4:00 p.m. Monday 14th January
Called into the triage room where the nurse advises me this is a police matter and it's arranged by Queensland Police Service (QPS), she was confused as to why I had presented in the emergency department, she asked me, 'who told you to present here?'

I told her how QPS had told me to go to my GP who then told me to come here. At this point I am in disbelief at the process so far, I am feeling extremely vulnerable, exposed and like I am in the wrong place... again.

The nurse left the room to speak with colleagues as she appeared unsure of how to proceed. When she returned, she called the local police station for clarity, she told them that she had a woman in emergency who has been the victim of a sexual assault and was told by QPS to attend emergency for a medical examination. I am unsure of the actual conversation that took place but when she hung the phone up, she told me that QPS will be sending a detective down.

Visibly distressed and emotional, I was ushered by the nurse into a small area where ambulance officers bring patients, the ambulance waiting area, I guess. I sat on a chair on my own in this public area sobbing, in front of two ambulance officers and a patient on a gurney waiting to enter the hospital. A concerned paramedic gave me a blanket, glass of water and suggested I sat in a small room close by for privacy, this is where I waited on my own for the officer to arrive. Deepest gratitude to that paramedic who went out of his way to assist me.

Recommendation 2 – Social workers must be available at the Emergency dept in hospitals for when victims of sexual assault present.

Social workers must be available to hospital emergency departments, when required. This is a highly traumatic experience in a very public environment, someone trained in psychological first aid is vital.

4:30 p.m. Monday 14th January

A plain clothed detective arrived, and introduced himself as a Senior Detective from the local station and apologised for the confusion. He advised me that there is someone specifically trained in conducting rape kits however, that person covers a large area regionally and is only in our hospital on specific days. Today was not a day that a trained worker could carry out a rape kit. So, unless you are raped on the day the trained worker is at your regional hospital, you miss out on the opportunity to have a rape kit done. Yep, that's right, read that last sentence again.

Recommendation 3 – Staff trained to conduct rape kits in hospitals

Multiple staff must be trained to conduct rape kits in regional hospitals and someone qualified must be available every single day. No rape victim should miss out on this vital step.

I remember saying to the detective while sobbing, 'I just want to go home,' and raising my voice in frustration saying, 'this is why women don't report, it's too hard!'

The detective offered support and empathy while explaining to me that it was up to me if I wanted to go ahead. Again, highlighting the difficult process victims go through and that it's often too hard for most victims. Conviction rates for sex crimes are really low and many women aren't able to complete this process. I know this information is given to a victim to allow them to make an informed decision but truly it just felt like I was being talked out of reporting, that it would most likely be a waste of time. I remember telling him that I had to, I couldn't not report as it would go against my morals and personal beliefs. As difficult as this was going to be, I had to report.

As I was unable to have a rape kit done, the detective arranged for a doctor from emergency to see me. As I stood naked in the cold sterile room, a doctor and nurse visually scanned my body documenting visible external injuries. Mainly bruising to my neck, chest and legs. No internal examination was offered and no rape kit conducted. The doctor and nurse were professional and respectful, the doctor told me he would be happy to appear in court and report his findings in person, if necessary.

The detective made an appointment with me for the next day to attend the police station to commence my official statement, he suggested I bring someone with me for emotional support.

6 p.m. Monday 14th January
I head home from the hospital. Driving home I am still in shock that I have been running around all day trying to report and have spent the past four hours at the hospital trying to get a medical done. Now I was heading home to my four children who have no idea what I have been through the past four days, thankfully they had spent the weekend at their dad's.

Time to pull myself together and put my happy face on, it's show time.

Chapter 4

Giving my Statement

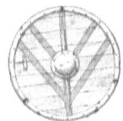

Tuesday 15th January

I knew I had to tell my older children in an age-appropriate way of course, but I really didn't want to tell them until the perpetrator had been arrested because I know the older girls would have been very scared and I didn't want to add any further unnecessary trauma. I was keen to get this statement out as quickly as possible. I tried my best to pretend all was normal and sent the kids off to school.

The next person I confided in was my good friend, ex-colleague and fellow social worker Kate. Kate is a beautiful and gentle soul who I felt safe with and given her profession, a suitable choice to have as a support person who ultimately has to hear the horrific details of what happened to me. Of course, Kate was more than happy to support me and came with me to the police station to meet with the detective and formally give my statement.

The detective conducted a quick search of the perpetrators history to see if there was any type of relevant history. There was in fact an incident recorded on his history involving an alleged rape when he was about nineteen. The perpetrator had walked a girl home from a local pub, at some point she had passed out. When she came to, he was on top of her, having sex with her. Clearly rape right? While the victim did report the incident to police like so many others she did not go through with prosecution. While there was a documented history of an alleged rape it was useless, he was never prosecuted, so it could not be mentioned in court.

Kate and I were due to play netball at 8 p.m. that night, so we arranged to be at the station at 5 p.m.. The detective met us downstairs in the foyer of the station and took us upstairs into an office where the three of us sat. The detective was in front of the computer typing, Kate and I sitting next to each other, linked arms and holding hands. I felt so much shame and embarrassment sitting there it was hard to get started. Both the detective and Kate were amazing during this process constantly reminding me that none of this was my fault and openly sharing their disgust and horror with my story. Kate is well known for her face of steel during difficult conversations, she is brilliant at it and even she broke down at times in disbelief.

At approximately 8:30 p.m. it was clear everyone needed a break. The detective suggested we come back tomorrow to finish the statement, but I needed it finished and we remembered we had netball. The detective encouraged us to go and play netball to take our mind off this for a bit and come back to finish it tonight. As strange as that sounds, this is what we did. We played netball,

Giving my Statement

I'm not really sure how I didn't cop a ball to the face to be honest from being distracted, thankfully I didn't.

The game finished and we headed back to the station to finalise the statement. The detective called my mum, who was home with my kids to let her know what was happening and that I would be home late. I gave permission for him to do so, he told my mum that I was the victim of a crime, that I was okay, and that I was just finishing off my statement and then would be home and would tell her all about it then.

We finalised my statement, the next step was to come back tomorrow to read and sign the final copy, conduct a photo board line up and conduct a video recorded phone call to the perpetrator from the police station, in the hope the perpetrator will admit what he did.

In the meantime, I was heading home to tell my mum. I knew I would also need the support of my brother and sister, so I sent them a text message asking them to meet me at my house to explain what happened as I only wanted to say it once. Kate offered to come home with me, but I assured her I would be fine, it had been a big day for both of us. We were physically and emotionally exhausted.

It must be about 10 p.m. when I arrive home with a copy of my statement in my hand. As I walk into the living area my family greet me with hugs, and we sit at my square eight-seater dining table. Keeping in mind they only know I have been the victim of a crime and that's it, they don't know any details. I really don't want to be here, I don't want to talk about this, my heart is pounding, but I know I must. At the table is myself, my mum, my sister with her husband, my brother with his wife. I sit there, at the table with my loved ones, seeing my families looks of concern and worry. I know this information is going to break their hearts. I tell everyone at the table that I didn't know how and what to say, so I tell them I am just going to read my statement out from beginning to end and to please wait until I'm finished to speak as I need to read it all out.

Through tears and moments of silence and overwhelm my family listened intently, without speaking, until I finished reading my statement. Every single person at that table was crying and visibly disturbed by what they had heard, hearing in detail what I had been through, how I had been violated, how I had been assaulted and how I had been raped. In hindsight this wasn't the best option as it was quite traumatic for my family to hear what had happened to their little sister, their daughter.

As soon as I finished speaking, I could see my mum desperately trying to say something and through tears she said,

'I need to say something, I need to say something, I am so sorry for what I said to you when you got home, the morning after, I'm so sorry, I should not have said that.'

I reassured her it was okay and that I was okay. I embraced each of my family members and we cried together. They all reassured me that they will support me and that we, as a family would get through this.

As hard as today was, I feel lighter, I feel like I have done my bit, I spoke my truth regardless of how it may make me look and I felt deep unconditional love and support from my family. Today is finally finished, I am utterly exhausted, my poor family and dear friend Kate, we are all trying to process what has happened.

Wednesday 16th January

I went back into the station with Kate, Mum, and my sister. My mum and sister met the detective, who filled them in on the process and next steps. I asked the detective if he wanted the messages from my phone, he explained to me that they have a program they run phones through to download content. He asked if there was anything on my phone I didn't want downloaded. I had nothing to hide and allowed QPS to download all the info on my phone. Turns out the defence would use text messages from my phone that I made to two other men I was chatting with around the same time and slut-shame me to the jury during the trial. A victim of a violent sexual assault could be having sex with multiple men at the same time, in fact, in today's dating world this is considered acceptable and a very normal dating practice. The victims sex life has nothing to do with consent and it certainly doesn't lessen the crime, it doesn't mean you consented, in fact it has absolutely nothing to do with the assault, it is straight up victim blaming. The perpetrators sex life isn't questioned, just the victims. The torch needs to move from the victims face and shone directly into the face of the perpetrator and nowhere else.

Recommendation 4 – Legal Representation must be mandatory right from the start

Victims of Sexual Violence must have their own legal representation who can advise them right from the moment of reporting and through until the trial is completed.

Don't Report Rape

The first I heard of the text messages being mentioned was about ten minutes before I took the stand as a witness. I had no time to even view the messages, I certainly didn't remember what may or may not have been said, we are talking about text messages sent over three years before. One man I had not even met and had no intentions of meeting, I just enjoyed chatting to him online. The other man I had been seeing casually. He was a nice guy, a bit quiet but someone I enjoyed hanging out with.

It is unreasonable and unjust to expect a victim to know and recall everything on their phone after a violent sex crime never mind her knowing what innocent information may or may not be used against her in court. I certainly was not able to do this. I didn't think I had anything incriminating on my phone and wanting the whole reporting side of things finished, I handed my phone over without a second thought. QPS should not be allowed to download a victim's phone unless the victim has received legal advice on this first. This would be considered a trauma informed approach as it would allow victims to make an informed decision on this matter. If I had not handed over my whole phone, my outcome in court would have been very different.

I made an appointment with the detective for later in the day to do the photo board line up and cold call.

Kate and I returned in the afternoon and were led into a different room, a room I hadn't been in before. There were TV's, desks and recording devices in this room. After we sat down the detective advised me, he was about to show me a photo board and that the process would be recorded in case it was needed in court. The detective placed a covered photo board in front of me and I was told to take my time and point out the perpetrator when identified. While I was confident that I would be able to identify

Giving my Statement

the perpetrator, I still had thoughts of *what if I don't recognise him? Or what if I pick the wrong one?* I took some deep breaths and held Kate's hand. The detective removed the cover revealing the photos, from memory I think there were eight photos of similar looking men. As soon as my eyes scanned the board, I recognised the perpetrator straight away and pointed to his picture. The detective confirmed on video the picture I had identified, and as expected, it was the perpetrator. While feeling relieved this bit was over, I was feeling very uncomfortable having to visually see his face and just wanted out of the room I was in.

Kate and I left and sat in the detective's office while he prepared that same recording room for the cold call. This was causing me high levels of anxiety and I wasn't sure I would be able to do it. Basically, after confirming that there had been no communication between the perpetrator and myself, of any kind since the assault, I was to now call him and just chat, tell him I wasn't into what he did, that I did not consent and that, he frightened me etc. This tactic is used to try to obtain a confession, so the conversation is recorded. Yep, I was absolutely crapping myself.

The detective takes us back to the recording room which is almost ready for the cold call. Kate and I are sitting at the table while the detective finalises a few things and leaves the room to get something he forgot. I have my phone in my hand and feel an incoming phone call, I look at my screen and see the perpetrator's name… what the fuck, he was calling me, why? *did he know I was in the police station? is this to intimidate me?* My fourteen-year-old self wonders… *is he just after another date, and doesn't think he did anything wrong, let alone criminal?* My heart was pounding, I showed my phone to Kate who saw that he was indeed calling. I asked her what to do, should I answer it? Where is the detective? We don't know what to do. I walked to the door and saw the detective, showed him the phone and he instructed me to answer it. Fuuuuuuuuuuuuuuck...... *OK, you got this Trish*, deep breaths. I sit down, I hold Kates hand while my other hand answered the call on speaker, 'Hello,' I said nervously. There was silence on the other end of the phone 'Hello,' I said again before the caller hung up. Given my state of mind at this point I had imagined all types of reasons why he was calling me, which frightened the hell out of me. The detective finished the set up and asked me to call him to see if he would answer. I called his phone, which rang out. The attempt at the cold call was unsuccessful. I was given a small recording device to carry on me and use if the perpetrator was to make contact.

The detective stated that he was going to send a referral for me to our local sexual assault support service. However, as I worked in the industry and knew a lot of the staff I wasn't comfortable accessing support through them and requested my referral go to a Sexual Assault Service in a neighbouring community who were able to provide immediate support via phone.

At this point, I'm a bit of a mess, it was late, and I just wanted to go home. I made another appointment for Friday to go into the station to read and sign my final statement. I headed home to put my happy mum face on and pretended nothing is wrong for my children.

Friday 18th January – One week since the assault

I went into the police station and met the detective as arranged. I read and signed my statement and was handed a copy for my own records. I asked the detective when realistically he thought he would be able to arrest the perpetrator. We spoke about how

Giving my Statement

I didn't want to tell my children until he was in custody. He told me that he hoped to do it on Sunday. I reminded him again that the perpetrator worked Monday to Friday and would not be home if you were to try during the week. At this point I am feeling extremely relieved, relieved my bit was done. I had reported an extremely violent sexual assault and now it was up to QPS. Just a few more days Trish, I told myself, just a few more days.

Chapter 5

The Arrest

Saturday 19th January

I created a private group of my friends (approximately 75 people) to keep everyone up to date with proceedings, for support and to help spread my message. I called the group My Tribe. This group of women came together with such force and fierceness, to stand with me, they supported me through some of my darkest days.

I have used some posts directly from that private group, so you can see exactly what this time was like, not only for me but also My Tribe. These women from all backgrounds, most strangers to each other responded collectively with anger, frustration, and disbelief.

Monday 21st January

My Tribe Update – Not having heard anything over the weekend I was hoping to hear that my perpetrator was arrested today.

Trish Fingers crossed today is the day my perpetrator is arrested

Wednesday 23rd January

My Tribe update – Email I sent to the detective today....
Time to make some noise ladies......

Today marks five days since I finalised my statement. In addition to my statement, I also identified the offender out of two photo board line ups, have a medical report supporting my statement as well as video footage of the offender checking into the motel where the crimes occurred.

I understand competing priorities however the women of our community are at risk. If our local police aren't manned enough to take into custody a violent predatory perpetrator, something is seriously wrong.
Hoping to hear something today.
Trish

Thursday 24th January

QPS attend his home however as I advised them, he works during the week and would not be home during working hours. The detective advised me that he spoke with the perpetrators mother who confirmed he was at work, the detective left a business card and asked the offender's mum to pass a message onto him to call the number on the card.

I can't help but feel like this was a poor attempt to arrest this perpetrator as they knew he was not going to be there and if I remember correctly the detective had leave booked starting the next day, 25th Jan. It appeared like they went to his home at this time to show they have attempted to arrest him so they can tick that box.

Friday 25th January

My Tribe Update – Just met with my team leader and service manager from work.
Two more amazing strong supportive women to add to my tribe.

Monday 28th January

My Tribe Update – the truth is there is no update, my detective is on leave and isn't due back until Friday. Yes, I am frustrated, scared, feel pushed aside, worry about the safety of myself and other women in the community. I know you all are frustrated and angry too BUT we need to stay positive, trust the process, trust the system and trust that justice will be served. I will continue to try to move on, to keep my happy face on for my children as I refuse to tell them until he is in custody. I will not be stuck in the shittyness of this process it will make me stronger. Next update hopefully Saturday. Keep comments positive, it will help me stay positive.

Don't Report Rape

Sunday 3rd February (3 weeks since the assault)

My Tribe Update – No update, no contact from QPS

Monday 5th February

My Tribe Update – First attempt back to work, struggling to hold my shit together..... chin up, wings out right?

Monday February 5th

My Tribe Update – OK so the good thing about the day is that I got up, got dressed and headed into work. The bad news is I didn't quite make it. I had a massive meltdown/panic attack in my car. Not an ideal start, but I tried....and I will try again.

Monday 5th February

My Tribe Update – GOOD NEWS UPDATE ....
Detective emailed saying he is planning to pick the perpetrator up tomorrow afternoon!!!!

It's happening!

Tuesday 6th February

My Tribe Update – Just got the call, he is in custody, goes before the magistrate in the morning

The Arrest

My Tribe Member - Praying for a good result in the morning

Trish Wyatt – the detective indicated they will not be opposing bail (not sure why, said it was the decision of the watch house) and that he will be released under strict bail conditions.

My Tribe Member – Trish wtf!!! The poor little sex offender was a good boy in the watch house, so we won't oppose bail. For what reason would you possibly not oppose bail for someone you are charging with sex offences!!! We could fill a book with all the reasons why women don't report sexual violence. Grrrr!!! Now that I've vented, how are you feeling about it?

Trish- numb.... and what's really fucked up is that I feel sorry for him, apparently, he cried...

My Tribe Member – Trish, clever little man showing them how sensitive and remorseful he is. Funny how they don't demonstrate the same sympathies to women when women cry. That big heart of yours. He knows how to work the system, Trish!

My Tribe Member – Trish did the detective tell you that?

Trish - the detective told me he was sobbing in the patrol car, and I said why would you tell me that? Am I supposed to feel sorry for him? He said no, I'm just telling you how he presented, said he was expecting a big macho man and didn't get that.

Wednesday 7th February

My Tribe Update – He has been charged with three offenses. Rape, sexual assault, and assault occasioning bodily harm.

Don't Report Rape

He was released on strict bail conditions, given time to seek legal advice and is due in front of the magistrate on 11th March.

Just to recap, it took QPS twenty days from the day I finalised my statement to arrest my perpetrator. He was kept in the watch house overnight and saw the magistrate in the morning. Bail was not opposed, I was told there is a certain criteria you must meet to be able to oppose bail and I was told in my case this was because he lived out of town, had a job and they didn't think the likelihood of me bumping into him in our regional town was high. I guess they didn't feel he was a risk in our community, he was released on bail.

Twenty days after my Statement was finalised, twenty days this violent perpetrator was left loose in our community. Twenty days he had opportunity to rape and assault more women. During these twenty days there were three weekends, three weekends with how many more possible victims? For me, the fact that it took QPS twenty days to arrest this man is absolutely disgusting. I understand competing priorities, sick leave, days off and holiday leave but if QPS can't manage their staff than they need more staff or more effective management of rosters. It's ridiculous that the detective that took the statement is responsible for the arrest, no one else could do it. So, because my detective was on leave, this perpetrator wasn't picked up until he returned? This makes no sense, police are supposed to protect, how exactly did my local police protect our community from this perpetrator? They didn't, he was free to roam for twenty days, to go about his business completely oblivious and quite possibly assaulting more women.

Meanwhile I am losing my mind, scared to leave the house, hypervigilant, experiencing panic attacks, nightmares and intrusive thoughts and the triggers... So many triggers; any sort of violence

The Arrest

on TV, men with neck tattoos, construction workers and the car seatbelt. The seat belt sat right on my neck, and I couldn't bare it, whenever it touched my neck I would find it hard to breathe and I would re-experience being strangled. I tried so many things, adjusting the belt, a belt cover, nothing worked, I tend to just hold it off my neck with one hand. I am going through all this trying to pretend all is well and keeping my happy face on for the sake of my children. For twenty days.

Recommendation #5 – QPS timing of arresting violent sex offenders

A review of procedures and policies is required, at least for my local police station, I am unsure how this relates to other police stations in the state. Surely, no one believes a violent rapist should be given free rein in our community for twenty days?

It is around this time that Jamie and I meet, everything clicked, he was perfect and everything I had ever looked for in a partner. I was nervous to tell my family because I knew that starting a relationship would really worry them, the timing wasn't great, and they are now really protective of me after what happened. I was very upfront with Jamie early on with regards to the assault and I had spoken to him about my family being cautious. Jamie suggested we have coffee with my mum and sister, so they can get to know him and know that I am safe with him. That's what we did, it was a little strange, not going to lie, felt like we were teenagers being grilled by parents. I am so glad we did, it certainly put my family at ease knowing I was being supported by this amazing man.

Chapter 6

The Assault

Standing in front of room 301 I nervously knock. The door opens. I quickly walk past the perpetrator who was holding the door open, put my bag down and put my drinks in the fridge. I feel a little overdressed, the perpetrator is wearing board shorts and a t-shirt.

We sit out on the balcony with our drinks and chat. The perpetrator pulled out a bowl of weed, puts it on his lap and starts chopping it up. We hadn't discussed drugs in any context, he really has no idea how I feel about it. I haven't smoked since I was a teenager, but I didn't have an issue with it. Chatting is going well, getting to know each other we spoke a lot about spirituality, he told me that he has been studying Buddhism. We talked about his tattoos and their meanings, a few spiritual ones, the chakras, a mandala and the eye of Horus. The tattoo that I was most intrigued with was a large chest piece that he showed me. It covered his full chest, without describing it in too much detail it represented good and evil by combining an angel and a devil. He told me it reminds him of the constant battle between good and evil.

We talk about music, and he tells me that he writes hip hop music and played me one of his songs. I got the impression that perhaps he had experienced trauma or hardship but had turned his life around. As time moves on, I am feeling less anxious and more excited, I'm enjoying his company, listening to the ocean, the smell of salt in the air, it's a beautiful summer night.

The perpetrator stood up and said he was going to the bathroom for a smoke and took his bowl of chop with him. I remained on the porch waiting for him to return. I was sitting directly in front of the door looking out at the ocean, so my back was to the door into the room. I didn't hear him coming back, so it startled me a little when I realised, he was standing right at the back of my chair, I could feel my heart pounding. I felt his gentle but firm hands on each side of my face as he tilted my head back, and passionately kissed me. This was an extremely intense and enjoyable first kiss, things were going great, the date was going great. We were getting along, had similar interests, laughing and drinking. I was feeling the joyful and relaxing effects of the alcohol. I felt safe and certainly hadn't experienced anything that indicated that I was in any sort of danger.

After the kiss, he sits back down in the chair that he was in before his smoke and we continue chatting, flirting, and laughing. More time passes and more alcohol is consumed. He gets up to have more weed and I ask if I can have some, not having had weed in about twenty years I was curious to try it again; he said yes, and we both went into the bathroom, and he shuts the door. He told me it's the only way to get around the smoke alarms. He grabbed

The Assault

a bong that he had stored in the bathroom cupboard under the sink and we both had a smoke. I felt an immediate lightheaded buzz, we kissed again in the bathroom and headed back to the balcony. The date is still going well, and I am still feeling enthusiastic and safe. While standing on the balcony we kiss some more, he turns me around to face the ocean, I leant on the top of the railing (which was solid concrete, so we were not visible to the public on the street) he discretely lifted my dress and we had consensual vaginal sex on the balcony, he used a condom. When he was on the stand in court, he said we didn't have sex on the balcony, that it simply just never happened. He said that he is not that type of person and would consider it to be disrespectful to the public who may see. What a load of shit, absolute shit and a total lie.

We fix ourselves up and sit back down on the balcony. It is right here, this is the moment, this is the turning point where my date goes from heaven to hell, from safe to life threatening and from enjoyable to painful. In hindsight, this is where I wished I thanked him for a lovely evening and left, but that's not what happened.

The perpetrator's body language and demeanour start to change. He lays back almost arrogantly in the chair and asked me, beside tonight, when was the last time I had sex. I try to dodge the question as I truly think he is joking, who would actually ask someone that, what does it matter? But it did to him, he was serious and was getting frustrated that I wasn't answering the question, I was feeling pressured to answer. I was becoming uncomfortable, and it felt like the type of conversation an exclusive couple would have if being accused of cheating, it was very weird. He leant forward over the table and looked me dead in the eyes and said,

'now, it's really really important you tell the truth, don't lie to me. I'll know. It's really important.'

Don't Report Rape

The laughing was gone, and I felt like I was being interrogated, I was uncomfortable, I said, 'last night.'

Now I know that probably wasn't a great answer and may have portrayed me as a slut, but I am an honest person and in my books honesty is the best policy regardless of whether it makes me look bad or not. He acknowledges my response silently.

'How about you?' I said.

'Three weeks ago.' He said.

He then starts making facial expression gestures to look like he was communicating with someone in a nearby building, I turn around to look but don't see anyone.

He said to me, 'what if I had a group of guys waiting to come over, they just needed the signal.'

I don't even remember what I said, I do remember feeling really confused and telling myself I'm being paranoid. It is around this time that my memories become a little harder to recall.

I find myself back in the bathroom with the perpetrator smoking pot. I remember I was leaning against the basin. I can't remember what we were talking about, but he tried to grab my neck, I moved my head.

He said, 'no, this is really important, I need to know what you can take, how tight.'

I shook my head no. He then swung his right hand back like he was going to slap me, as his hand swung towards my face, I raised my

The Assault

left arm up and blocked it from hitting me, I said no, and started to leave the bathroom. He followed me and threw me on the bed, I landed on my back and before I knew it, the perpetrator had climbed on top of my body, his full weight of approximately eighty kilograms is on my chest, each knee pins both my shoulders and arms down, he leans forward and rapes me orally. This position had me trapped, frightened unable to move and seriously struggling to breathe. The weight of his body on my chest was crushing and the airways from my nose were covered by his skin and body, I remember panicking while his penis was forced into my mouth struggling to breathe so I tried to open my mouth as wide as I could to get air in. This was forceful, rough, and certainly not pleasant or enjoyable for me, I was terrified. This was the only time this technique was used. During the trial this incident is referred to as *The oral incident* and is the first rape charge.

Before I know it, he has climbed down to a kneeling position, I am on my back, he rapes me vaginally. This is all happening extremely fast I didn't even see his hand coming the first time he hit me with an open hand across the face and in a split second while penetrating me I felt the sting on my face as my whole head swung from one side to the other followed by both of his hands tightening around my neck, restricting my breathing. What the fuck is happening. So confused. *Shit, what have I got myself into. What the hell do I do.*

I lost count of how many times he hit and strangled me while penetrating as it happened over and over during the evening. This particular incident in the trial is referred to as *the vaginal rape* and is the second count of rape as well as the first and only count of assault occasioning bodily harm.

I am wanting to run, to leave, to fight, to scream but I can't. *Come on Trish, I tell myself, just get up. Just go.* But my body was unable to move. I am frozen. I am too scared to say or do anything to make him angry. The only way I was going to escape this alive was to go along, pretending everything is fine. I talk about this like it was a cognitive decision I made but it really wasn't, it was my automated stress response, something I had no control over.

He then flips me over onto my knees with my back to him as he grabs me from behind, around the neck and puts me in a choke hold. Out of all the things that happened that night, this is the most terrifying, this is where I questioned my mortality, this is when I thought I might die, this is when I wonder if I will ever see my children again. I knew with one small move he could snap my neck, tears stream down my face. While in this position, he rapes me anally. This incident is referred to as *The anal rape* and the third rape charge. The choke hold attracts the first assault charge.

I vividly remember leaving my body, just like the fourteen-year-old me did all those years ago. If you haven't experienced this, it's quite difficult to explain. You actually leave your body and watch the events like a third person, an observer, like watching a movie. This is another automated trauma response, it's not a decision made by a victim. Your brain decides this is too horrific for you to experience and forces you out of your body for protection.

There was a second assault charge for what is extremely difficult to describe and causes me to feel ill just thinking about it. Basically, he tried to use his hands to stretch my vagina. Now, I have birthed four children and I am sure a lot of mothers out there know the pain and discomfort of the good old 'stretch and sweep'. A technique performed by a gynaecologist when baby is overdue to induce labour. This is not an enjoyable experience and in fact was extremely painful. Just so we are all on the same page, it's probably best if you imagine what someone would look like if they

The Assault

were trying to open a train or elevator door manually with their hands, fingers in, palms facing away from each other, elbows out, now apply force. It would appear this was in preparation for his next sex crime.

Commonly known as fisting. The perpetrator tried to forcefully insert his fist into my vagina. This particular act attracted a lot of attention when I was being cross examined by the defence in court. I was pushed into describing intricate details for approximately thirty minutes on this one act. The defence even wanted to change the definition as she didn't think it fitted the description of fisting. I ended up saying the f word in court and looking to the judge desperately who called for a break and instructed the defence to move on. The criminal charge for this rape was attempted rape referred to in court as *The fisting incident.*

It honestly felt like he got some type of enjoyment inflicting pain while having sex. He would even do things like dig his elbow into my chest and move it slowly across my chest, just to cause pain. During the violent sexual incidents there is no talking, I only recall a few things he said which were, 'fucking take it,' and 'I make the rules.'

The next rape charge relates to me being asleep. I woke up to the perpetrator on top of me penetrating me vaginally with the same violent routine I had seen so many times that night. Forceful open-handed hits across the face and strangulation. Referred to in court as *The sleeping rape.*

Now let's summarise these charges:

1 Rape – Oral
1 Rape – Vaginal

Don't Report Rape

1 Assault Occasioning Bodily Harm – Strangulation
1 Rape – Anal
1 Assault – Choke hold
1 Assault – Stretching
1 Attempted Rape – Fisting
1 Rape – Sleeping

So, that's four rape charges, two assault charges, one attempted rape and one assault occasion bodily harm. Eight sex crimes in total. Even though these crimes occurred multiple times a charge can only be applied when a specific incident or act can be isolated and described. Even though there are only eight charges I feel confident, and I still hear the words of the detective, 'We only have to get him on one.' If only this was the case.

Chapter 7

2018 First Year Waiting for Trial

7th February

The day my perpetrator was arrested was the day I tried to explain to my two eldest daughters aged twelve and ten at the time. How the fuck was I going to do this? How do I look into their innocent eyes and tell them this? They knew something bad had happened, something that changed their mum, something that causes her to sleep a lot and something that causes her to cry a lot. I kept it brief and just said that I was hurt by a man I met for a date and that the man who did it, has been arrested by police and has been charged. I assured them we were safe. I explained to them that the event has really shaken me up and impacted my mental health which is why I cry and sleep a lot. I explained this is why Grandma is living with us to help out and I assured them that I am getting help through support services and doctor's and that I am going to be okay.

8th February

After spending the previous night in the local Watch House, the perpetrator appeared for the first time in front of the Magistrate. He was released on bail with strict conditions not to make any contact with me. He was given time to access legal support and was due back in court on 11th March 2018.

12th February

Today was my second attempt at returning to work which was really difficult. While I was on maternity leave a lot had changed. A lot of colleagues I use to work with had now left, our office was relocated to the main office which meant lots more colleagues and a completely new working environment. Beside my team leader and manager (who were away on the day I returned) I really only knew one person and everyone else were strangers. I was very anxious and feeling very vulnerable. Unable to keep my emotions in check, I left early.

The role I returned to was in Intensive Family Support. Our team received referrals, mainly from Child Safety for us to provide intense in-home support for families experiencing abuse and neglect. Additionally, these families had multiple and complex issues including drug and alcohol misuse, mental health, trauma, various types of abuse and domestic violence. We would do this through building rapport with families in a non-judgemental trauma informed framework. The aim of our service was to increase the children's safety at home by working through these issues with parents and the family as a whole with various parenting strategies, psychological education, advocacy and specialist referrals when needed. It was tough work and required me to attend the homes of the families we supported.

My team leader and service manager were amazing and a wonderful example of how an employer can support a member of staff through something like this. They were very flexible with my hours; I was allowed to come and go as I needed. If I had a panic attack, I could just go home and felt supported to do so. Struggles with work started to appear fairly quickly. I certainly didn't feel comfortable conducting home visits, which was the main duty of my role. However, I was given jobs that allowed me to remain in the office. I had trouble reading referrals as they often contained violence and stories of terrible trauma. It would remind me of the trauma I had been through with intrusive memories of the assault randomly popping into my head which was overwhelming.

20th February

With the support of the organisation and management, I temporarily moved out of the heaviness of the Intensive Family Support role and into the Fostering team for three months as an assessment writer. It was a relief to step back from the front line. My new role involved me interviewing potential foster carers and writing a report if I recommended them to be approved as foster carers. I had worked in foster care when I was in Roma, so I was familiar with the work.

My Tribe Update – When I first returned to work, I wondered if I would ever be able to return to social services but now, I am so optimistic, I can do this, and I will do this. I have had two great full days. Feeling strong and positive!

11th March

My Tribe Update – The perpetrator appeared in the local Magistrates court with his partner. I was not required to attend however, my mum, brother, brother-in-law and friends Angela and Cristel did attend. He didn't say a word and made no plea. Police Prosecutors were instructed to provide all evidence to his lawyer by 15th April 2018. The next step is a Committal mention set for 2nd May 2018. He will now have access to my statement and version of events and decide how he will plea. The process has begun.

1st April

Being out in public is really difficult, I started feeling really paranoid that people were staring at me, that maybe they knew the perpetrator, had seen my photos and recognised me along with thoughts of what if I bumped into him. The anxiety around this prevented me from going out in public on my own. I decided to change my hair colour in an attempt to be less recognised and to feel safer in the community.

My Tribe Update – Feeling safer out in public and less anxious since changing my hair. Changed from wavy blonde back to straight, dark brown.

2nd May
My Tribe Update – My case was mentioned in court on 2nd May and adjourned to the 13th of June.

2018 First Year Waiting for Trial

Me – I'm ok, it is what it is, I'm prepared for a tough and long battle. I have recently been diagnosed with Complex Post Traumatic Stress Disorder (PTSD), and I'm in the process of changing medications. I have found a great psychiatrist and trauma counsellor.

Despite my smiling face which I was great at, inside was dark. My day-to-day life was extremely hard. I was finding myself being hypervigilant, in an elevated state of constantly assessing for potential danger. Being overly alert and on the lookout all the time is exhausting. I found sleep a fantastic coping mechanism early on as it basically allowed me to escape reality however, I was also experiencing nightmares, calling out and fighting in my sleep as well as waking up startled and frightened. At this point I have continued to see my GP who referred me to a psychiatrist who formally diagnosed me with complex PTSD, major depression and anxiety as a direct result of the assault. I commenced medication to treat these conditions immediately. I also started seeing a psychologist twice a week.

Even with my new role at work, I was still finding it difficult. I was having issues with my focus and concentration. I would find myself reading the same line over and over or I would finish reading something and not remember what I just read. The physical exhaustion left me struggling to keep my eyes open sitting at my desk. I felt so lost, nothing I was experiencing was familiar to me and I found myself sinking deeper and deeper into a black hole. I paused my return to work and checked myself into The Health Retreat on the Sunshine Coast Queensland, a five-hour drive from my home. On top of work struggles I had massive mother guilt. I knew I couldn't be the mother to my children that I was prior to the assault, I tried so hard, but I just couldn't. I had very little patience and slept all the time.

At home, things were strained. My eldest daughter was struggling with seeing me unwell as well as understanding the separation of her parents who had now both moved on with new partners. My mum was a great help at this time as I just didn't have the clarity or strength at times to address the conflict between my daughter and me.

16th May

My Tribe Update – After a rapid decline in my mental health, I have booked into a residential mental health retreat on the sunny coast. 15 days of intense psychotherapy and natural therapies. I check in tomorrow.
- not sure how I'll go with the no caffeine, no dairy, and no wheat but I'll give it a go.

There is a great balance of medical and natural therapies, and the clinicians specialise in various modalities, so you can explore which one suits you best.

The retreat was amazing, and I am so glad I went. It is located deep in the beautiful Sunshine Coast mountains. The facilities were amazing and the space in general was peaceful. When arriving you are given your weekly schedule which is jam packed of various activities. I had a private room located right next door to the office to increase my sense of safety. All the staff are extremely friendly and helpful. Every day starts off with physical exercise, either a walk on the beach or hike in the mountains. Programs are individually designed to include 30 hours a week to group psychoeducation, designed to change the neural pathways and consolidate new ways of thinking. You learn real skills on how to address uncomfortable or negative thinking, memories, triggers, and feelings in a safe and supported environment instead of numbing everything out with medication and hiding under the doona, which was becoming my go to treatment.

There is yoga, drumming, organic cooking, tapping, acupuncture, Chinese medicine, massage, cupping, three-day juice detox, swimming, sauna, campfires. As well as private sessions with a general practitioner (GP), psychologists and an amazing naturopath.

The retreat encourages family members to attend any of the group day programs with you to help them understand what you are learning to help and support your recovery; your visitors eat for free. I was hopeful to bring home some new coping strategies I could teach my eldest daughter and help repair our currently fractured relationship.

Family members are welcome to stay with you overnight in your room at no extra charge. Jamie came down and spent the weekend with me which was amazing. My Uncle and Aunty who live on the Sunshine Coast came to visit and had lunch with me. My brother attended a day session and had dinner with me.

Lifetime Bonus – having been part of the program, I can access day programs for free whenever I like in the future, including food!

This retreat was truly transformational, it's just a shame I had to travel five hours to get there, something like this which is basically a holistic trauma informed healing centre is desperately needed in my regional community and I imagine most regional towns.

22nd May

My Tribe Update – one week in update...
I'm so glad I decided to come here, it's been amazing, and I still have a week to go. My daily schedule is pretty busy from 8.30 to 5.30 with not much down time, so I have been working really hard and making really good progress. The detox from caffeine and sugar was tough but that's behind me now. I have more energy, feel lighter, head clearer, working through triggers and trauma from the assault.
So far, I have had sessions with psychologists, doctor, naturopath, counsellors, inner journey work, blood tests, beach/forest walks, two seminars each day, deep tissue and relaxation massages and cupping therapy hurt like hell but feeling better for it.
Missing the kids terribly but just one more week to go.

4th June

My Tribe Update – two weeks and home update: well, I'm back home and settling back into 'normal' life. I was so impressed with the retreat and would highly recommend it for anyone stuck in depression, anxiety, PTSD or addiction.

I worked really hard while I was there and I'm feeling positive about my recovery. My mind is clear and I'm feeling stronger than ever. The change in medication seems to be working well too.
PS next court mention is next Thursday

13th June

My Tribe Update – no surprises, another adjournment was granted. Next court mention is 25th July. Thank you to my Mum, my Brother and Angela for attending court and keeping me updated.
After returning from the retreat, I started back at work on reduced hours which seemed to be going OK.

25th July

My Tribe update – another adjournment to the 22nd of Aug. My case has now moved from the magistrate's court to the district court due to the seriousness of the crimes. No plea has been made. Perpetrator did not attend today. While it's another adjournment, it's a step in the right direction and just the process. At least it will be heard in the appropriate court. One step closer.

22nd August

My Tribe Update – Adjourned to 11th November for an indictment.

29th August

Getting back to work still wasn't progressing. I was still struggling with focus and concentration. I wasn't feeling very productive. I started to feel like I was wasting everyone's time. I had tried for eight months. Despite continued support from the organisation and management I resign from work to focus on my healing. I felt like a failure.

September

I filed for divorce and obtained legal representation to commence property settlement with my ex-husband.

October – Ryder almost drowned

It was a beautiful spring afternoon; Jamie and I were at home with the kids getting dinner ready. It must have been about five when we heard screams from my eleven year old daughter Violet, she had been watching tv in my room. My room overlooked the backyard.

'RYDER IS IN THE POOL! RYDER IS IN THE POOL!'.

I frantically start running to the back door, Jamie is running in front of me. I will never forget the sight of Ryder, face down in the pool. Jamie jumped in and pulled Ryder out. After seeing Ryder in the pool, I remember standing at the pool gate frozen, feeling urine running down my leg, I no longer had control of my body. I didn't want to go any closer, I was too scared.

2018 First Year Waiting for Trial

Thinking the worst as I ran inside to call an ambulance. On the phone to triple zero arranging an ambulance I drop to my knees in distress unable to stand. At this point I don't know how long he had been in there.

I could hear Jamie yell out, 'it's okay, he is breathing, it's okay.'

The older kids came over to me saying,

'it's okay, Mum, he is okay, he is breathing.'

Jamie brings him to me wrapped up in towels and I hold him until paramedics arrive.

Turned out Violet had thought she heard a splash when she was watching TV, she said something inside her told her to look out the window, so she did and that was when she saw Ryder. She is a true hero, had she not listened to her intuition I have no doubt Ryder would have drowned that day. We were living in a rental property at the time, and we were unaware the pool gate was faulty and didn't always latch when it was closed. We contacted the real estate, and they fixed the gate immediately, we moved out of that house not long after.

As soon as I arrived at the hospital I called my ex-husband, Ryder's father. God this was a call I really didn't want to make but I knew it was the right thing to do. I told him what had happened and that we were at the hospital. He told me he was staying at his partners place that night which was not far from the hospital in case he needed to come in urgently. Ryder was observed overnight in hospital and thankfully we were released in the morning with no issues. Doctors didn't believe he was in the water long which matches with the splash Violet heard.

Medical staff praised what a hero his big sister was. Violet truly saved his life.

19th November

My Tribe Update -The indictment (formal list of charges) was presented at the District court on Mon 11/11/18.
The next court date will be a mention in Bundaberg District Court, date yet to be determined. Perpetrator has made no plea.
There may be a number of mentions before a hearing date is set. The DPP in Brisbane will advise me when a hearing date is set.

Chapter 8

2019 Second Year Waiting for Trial

11th January

My Tribe Update – Today marks one year ...
1 year since I was brutally assaulted, raped and strangled.
1 year since my world as I knew it, fell apart.
1 year since I thought I was going to die.
1 year since I thought I may never see my children again.
1 year since the most frightening, confusing, terrifying, humiliating, and degrading experience of my life...

Since then, I have been healing and rebuilding and I'm proud of how far I have come. I have discovered an inner warrior and strength within that I didn't know I had. I am inspired and excited

to share my story, to change cultures and look into ways to improve the processes of reporting, to make a difference.
Court update: The DPP advised me yesterday that the next mention is listed for March 16th, 2019.

24th March

During my time off work, I focused on mindfully acknowledging everything that came up for me; triggers, negative thoughts and unpleasant emotions. I wasn't really connecting with the psychologist I was seeing so I tried a new one. I truly believe that it is really important you don't give up on therapy if you are not clicking with a therapist, finding a therapist is like buying a car, you need to find the right one for you. I was later referred to an amazing psychologist, who I was seeing regularly. We did some great work and after about six months off work I was feeling ready to re-enter the workforce. I had come across an advertisement for our local youth refuge, I accepted the role and commenced full time work. It felt great, the site was highly secure with swipe cards to enter rooms and cameras that covered the entire site. I was upfront with management about the assault and my upcoming court proceedings they were very supportive and understanding. I felt confident in the role and felt an asset to the team.

26th March

My Tribe Update – The DPP advised me today that the mention was not heard in the district court this week and has been scheduled to May.

2019 Second Year Waiting for Trial

19th May

My Tribe Update – The May court date has been cancelled. No date set yet. The DPP will let me know when a court date is set.

My two eldest daughters are still refusing to see their dad and only maintain minimal contact via text. They both experienced this time of their lives very differently; my eldest shows her emotions externally and Violet withdraws and quietly goes within. Both behaviours are very concerning and both girls commenced therapy addressing issues around the divorce and their relationship with their dad.

26th June

Despite my committed attempt to get back into the work force, it all came crashing down about two and a half months into the role when I found myself in a violent and potentially harmful situation with a young person in the office. The refuge is a two-story building with the main refuge space upstairs. I was the only staff member upstairs at the time and my manager, was in his office downstairs, where he can view all security cameras. We had a young person highly distressed, erratic and possibly under the influence. He had been at the refuge a few weeks and I had established a good rapport with him. To remove any threat to the other people present, I was sitting in the office with him trying to help regulate him. There was a panic button in there in case it is needed.

The young person started raising his voice, hitting the wall and pushed a chair over. I was sitting right in front of the security camera. I knew my manager heard the noise and would be looking at the cameras to see what was going on. I am not too sure what my thinking was at this point I just remember feeling stuck, frozen and scared. I remember looking into the camera trying to communicate telepathically with him, to tell him I needed help. Crazy I know, but that's how it happened. I could literally see the big round red panic button from where I was sitting. I just couldn't move. I am saying to myself get up, get up, just GET UP AND PRESS THE FUCKING BUTTON. I even had the work mobile phone in my hand. It was in my hand, and I couldn't use it to ring for help. Is all this sounding familiar? Well, it should because it's another example of an automatic trauma response.

Luckily my manager was watching what was happening and even though what he was watching on camera didn't indicate anything too serious, he still phoned the mobile I was holding just to check if everything was okay. As soon as I heard the phone ring and saw it was my manager, I answered the phone like a normal incoming call to the refuge. My manager said,

'hey Trish, is everything ok?'

I was only able to reply with one word, 'no.'

He assured me it's ok, he is getting help. He called police and came straight up to the office.

This was devastating for me. This was a situation that I would have managed completely different prior to the assault, a situation I had experience in and had felt confident in. Not anymore. Despite having all the safety measures, cameras, panic button and a phone in my hand my trauma response of freezing won. Despite the work I had done in therapy, despite a change in role, a change into a highly secure environment… none of it mattered.

2019 Second Year Waiting for Trial

I still froze, not by choice I know, but that was the outcome for me when faced with a threat. I felt hopeless, I felt like I may never work again. I resigned from the youth refuge and have not returned to the workforce since. That was my last job in social services.

26th June

My Tribe Update – I have decided to leave work and now need to consider options outside of social services, possibly any work involving the public.

A few weeks ago, I was involved in an incident with a young person at the refuge ...
This has brought up a lot of confusing thoughts and painful memories. I'm angry that my perpetrator has changed who I was. It's like there was one version of me before the assault who was a confident professional and connected mother and one version of me after the assault who is basically faking it, frightened and withdrawn. I'm angry and sad that I may never see the old me again and that I can't pursue my choice in career which I'm so passionate about, have put so much into and know I was good at.

Just feels all pretty fucked up really, thanks for listening, I have great support, Jamie is amazing, and I have reconnected to my psychiatrist and psychologist.

While listening to my favourite radio station Triple J, I heard journalist Avani Dias talking about increases in sexual assaults particularly with online dating and Triple J along with Four Corners were planning a joint investigation. They were asking people with experience to send personal stories in. This was right up my ally. I wrote to Avani telling her my story who called me to chat. She was extremely empathic and shocked by how similar my story was to so many other stories she had heard. Avani had stated she would love to come to my home with a camera crew and conduct some interviews. Before confirming I could participate in this project, I wanted to seek some legal advice first, as I didn't want to jeopardise my case. I spoke with the DPP who advised me to get legal advice, which I did, and that advice was not to participate in anything until the trial was over as it may cause a mistrial.

Victims are gagged from speaking publicly about their assaults. So, not only are victim's lives put on hold waiting years for a trial, but they aren't allowed to talk about it. Both of these things contribute to preventing the victim from moving on and keeps them in this stagnant and cruel space of waiting… just waiting. Reluctantly, I advised Avani that I was unable to proceed with the interview as I was not prepared to jeopardise my case.

1st October

My Tribe Update – Unfortunately I have had to decline to participate in the Triple JJJ/Four corners investigation as its too risky for my case.

On a positive note, I did get a call from the lead detective to let me know I should be getting a trial date soon. Possibly in the October 2019 sitting but most likely Jan or Feb next year.

22nd October

My Tribe Post – Devastated! I was hoping for a trial date at today's mention in the district court, however, the defence stated they were not ready for the trial. The judge granted an adjournment until February 2020 when it's listed for another mention. I have no words.

I initiated mediation with the Family and Relationship Centre (FRC) to help repair the relationship between the eldest two children after they had started to refuse to visit their Dad. However, after many appointments and the stress I was under with the criminal trial, the FRC deemed it no longer appropriate to continue with mediation and advised us to proceed with legally supported mediation.

30th November

My Tribe Court Update -The DPP called me today and advised they have changed the charges from three to eight. Apparently, this was done 12 months ago at the indictment on 11th November 2018 however I was not advised. This was the first time I had heard of the charges changing. Originally the offender was charged with x2 counts of rape and x1 count of assault. Now, however, he has been charged with eight crimes.

X5 counts of rape
X1 common assault
X1 assault occasioning bodily harm
X1 Attempted rape.

DPP stated that they did look at a torture charge but didn't feel they had enough evidence.

He advised me that the defence is preparing for trial. Hopefully get a trial date in the February 2020 sitting. Bit overwhelmed and *emotional, trying to process it all but overall, its good news and a step forward.*

Domestic Violence Court v Criminal Court

The victim's relationship with the perpetrator or lack of, determines what court and what laws your case will be heard. As I didn't have a prior relationship with my perpetrator, my case fell under criminal law. The problem with this, is that strangulation is recognised as a standalone crime under Domestic Violence Law however this is not the case with criminal law. It simply falls into assault.

> **Recommendation 6 –** Strangulation must be a stand-alone crime
>
> **Strangulation laws that are current under domestic violence laws, need to be included in criminal law. Strangulation is strangulation. Someone puts their hands around your throat, tightens their grip to prevent you from breathing, without consent. It IS A CRIME if you are in a relationship with the offender but NOT A CRIME if it's a stranger?**

Hearing the eight charges was very overwhelming and it stirred up a lot of feelings. It did wonders for my healing as it validated my experience, it validated that those crimes did occur, horrific crimes as determined by our laws. It would have been more beneficial to my recovery to have known this sooner. I am unsure why I wasn't advised of the change in charges or who was responsible for advising me of this.

2019 Second Year Waiting for Trial

Recommendation 7 – DPP accountability and wait time for trial

Whilst keeping victims up to date with their case is current policy and stated as such in the 'Charter of Victims Rights', this did not happen for me. I was not advised in November 2018 when the charges were changed, I was advised one year later. Something is wrong with processes or procedures that allowed this to occur. A victim having to wait over 3 years for a trial is unacceptable and needs to be rectified immediately.... This may be more judges, prosecutors , courtrooms, admin staff, monthly sittings for regional communities instead of bimonthly... what ever is required to reduce this time must be done.

This year has been tough, my two eldest still refuse to visit their dad and are accessing therapy. My mental health still isn't great. Sometimes when I am driving my surroundings seem completely unfamiliar and I panic that I am lost. I wake up like this too sometimes, not recognising my bedroom and thinking I am somewhere else. I am struggling daily with triggers and negative thoughts, I feel numb, like I have sunk into a deep black hole, and I really don't know if I can get out of it. I have often thought about the women who have taken their own lives waiting for trial and I can totally relate. There is a desperate need for the pain and suffering to end, for it to just stop, despite doing all the right things like taking medication and actively working through therapy. While at times, I did have suicidal thoughts and regularly experienced overwhelming feelings to just run away. I didn't, and I credit this to the support I had from family and friends particularly Jamie. I am thankful that I had an entire fucking cheer squad supporting me and holding me up.

Chapter 9

2020 Third year waiting for trial

11th January

My Tribe Post – Two-year anniversary. Today marks two years since I was assaulted. It's funny, people say 'how are you doing' or ' you're all good now though'. Most of the time, I just smile and say, 'getting there'. I simply don't have the heart to tell people how this single act of violence has impacted negatively on my life, my sense of identity, my parenting and general functioning as a human being. Truth is, I'm pretty fucked up, but I'm a fighter and I will continue fighting. I am grateful to be surrounded and supported by my friends, family and my amazing fiancé.
Fingers crossed we get a trial date soon

15th March

The March4Justice movement was happening nationally, and I encouraged tribe members to attend their local event. On this day 110,000 women and our allies marched at over 200 events in Australia. This was a fantastic outcome, society standing up and supporting victims.

My Tribe Update – Dear Tribe, I truly hope you were able to get to the march4justice event in your area, now is the time, women are gathering Australia wide. Local friends, ours is tonight:

4.30 March from the courthouse
Wear black, bring signs, bring the men and young people in your lives. If the men who run our country aren't held accountable, what hope do I /we have.

Whilst this was hugely successful nationally and attracted the attention of the media, the turn out locally was really disappointing, and I took it personally. I was pissed off. I couldn't understand how this wasn't an issue important enough to get people out of their houses. I just couldn't understand it. I spoke with my sister about it trying to work out why people didn't show up. We concluded that perhaps it's still a taboo subject, a subject that makes people feel uncomfortable a subject society has a hard time accepting and perhaps people prefer to stick their head in the sand. Everyone has a mother, possibly a sister or sister-in-law, friends, colleagues, and daughters. Are the statistics not bad enough? I realised this wasn't personal, sadly it's just our society. People seem happy to bitch and whine about issues but aren't prepared to contribute to making change.

My family and just a few friends attended. We brought along my home-made signs, various people spoke including myself and

2020 Third year waiting for trial

my twelve-year-old daughter Violet who spoke beautifully with the support of her cousin standing beside her. She told the crowd how proud she was of me for speaking my truth and fighting for justice, it was an emotional moment. We ended up getting rained out, but it was still a great event to be a part of.

26th March

My Tribe update – The pretrial hearing was yesterday, the defence requested access to my medical records. The Judge has allowed the DPP to access my medical records to analyse and determine what is relevant. Another pretrial hearing listed for May. This process is so cruel for the victim, every mention, every adjournment, every pretrial hearing and every phone call in-between. Constant re-traumatising, constantly hanging over your head while you try to 'get on with your life'.

All for just a three percent conviction rate!
I will not withdraw, no matter what comes my way. I will fight to the end.

31st May

My Tribe Update – Why it's important to speak up!
Back in March I was horrified with the way our Catholic High School Principal (the school my children attended) was addressing consent with students. It was full of victim blaming language, no trigger warning and certainly was not trauma informed. I addressed this with the principal who didn't think he had done anything wrong and justified everything he said. So, I took my concerns higher, to the Catholic diocese and while they agreed with my concerns and promised professional development for principals and external programs to educate students, I wasn't too hopeful. Well today an email about consent was sent out by the same principal and it's a complete turnaround from what was sent out three months ago. It was a great example of how this issue needs to be addressed and included all my recommendations. Would this change have occurred without my complaint? Who knows....but

2020 Third year waiting for trial

I am claiming it. I feel so proud. After feeling so down, defeated, and unheard for so long, today is a great day. I have shown my children why speaking up is so important.
Change is possible.
Knowing how important positive feedback is as well, I emailed the diocese letting them know how great the communication was written and to pass on my thanks to everyone involved in making the change. Below is part of their reply.

'It is only by people speaking up that we will change our systems, how men treat women, how boys treat girls and so much more – but it takes a lot of courage to do so! So, thank you for having this courage!'

Thank you to the teachers who also fought to address this issue and showed compassion and empathy, not only to me but to my daughters.

(Cue happy tears)

Tribe Member Comments
'This is so amazing. Thank you for speaking up. Next time I feel scared to speak up, I will think of this.'

'Today is a bloody great day, Trish. You stand, you breathe, you fight, your flame is bright.'

'So proud of you Trish. Change can't happen without courageous people like you, well done cous xx'

'That is truly amazing Trish, you are an inspiration. What an impact you have had and will continue to make !! xx'

'This is so wonderful Trish and what an inspiration for your girls. Your making real positive change to an outdated system.'

'You are amazing! So proud to be your friend, your strength has always had me in awe and your resilience in coping with what's happened to you brings tears to my eyes. You're my hero and a hero for all women, I love you.'

'I love to hear about your resilience, strength and determination Trish, you are a true inspiration. Thank you for what you are doing to help so many xx'

31st May

My Tribe Update – call over is on Thursday. High chance of getting a trial date, which could be as early as 14th June

3rd June

My Tribe Update – Absolutely devastated......... earliest court date now NOVEMBER!!!!.......shattered....... And they wonder why victims don't report, And they wonder why victims suicide before getting to trial..... it's fucking terrible. That's almost three years since the assault! Don't worry, I'll be fine, I have great support. Until November.

Jamie and I were due to celebrate our wedding in August, however as it was apparent that the trial would not occur before then, we decided to cancel our wedding and reschedule it for October 2022. I really didn't want the lingering trial hanging over our heads on what is going to be the happiest day, celebrating love with family and friends.

4th June

My Tribe Update – Reasons for the delay in getting to trial ......
First up, a woman raped in regional Queensland doesn't receive the same process for justice as a woman raped in Brisbane. This is because we live in a regional community and are on a circuit court, this means district court only sits every second month. As opposed to cities who have sittings continuously. As well as that everyone needs to be available for any suggested date. All witnesses, the detective who I reported to as well as the perpetrator and his team etc, this can be tricky with only six opportunities for a trial each year. Secondly, at the last pre-trial hearing on 21st May. The judge recommended to the DPP that they should get a medical report to support the case. Had the DPP arranged this straight away, we would have been ready for the June sitting and at that time there was still space for a trial. However, the DPP didn't request this report until the 31st ^{of} May 2020, 10 days later. Why? I have no idea. They allocated the free space in the June sitting to another case. I asked questions like

- *are there any other cases that involve a violent/sex crime as old as my case?*
- *were the 4 cases that got the June sitting for violent/sex crimes?*
- *had the report been requested straight away, would we have been ready for June.*
- *is there priority given to the type of crime/impact on victim?*
- *what happens if we don't get a trial date in November? As court doesn't sit December and January. This would mean at least February 2021 (over three years).*

Not a lot of direct answers were given just a lot of beating around the bush.

With June being out, the next option was Aug when Jamie and I were due to be married so I had said I was unavailable for Aug, Sept one falls in school holidays and not everyone available. Which leaves Nov.

I expressed my desperation, disappointment and anger with the system while trying not to hyperventilate and articulate my words clearly. The DPP said they understand my frustration and there isn't much that can be done. Once dates are allocated that's it, they can't be changed. They did suggest we apply to have my case heard in Brisbane but the process for that would probably be just as long. If only this was suggested in 2018 when there was already a two-year wait for trial and that was before delays from covid. Jamie suggested just doing the trial in Aug ... I just don't think I could do it. It would mean the trial was either days before the wedding, days after or even still in progress over the weekend of the wedding. I just need to find a way to keep going. Everyone says how bad the system is QPS and DPP but why is it still like this? Do we need more judges, more court rooms, more lawyers? Women taking their life waiting for trial still isn't enough for the 'law makers' to change things. How many more women need to die for them to make change?

21st June

My Tribe Update – I have been advised by the DPP that my Trial Date will be 1st November 2020. It's happening, just need to get through 4.5 months. The November sitting in the District court starts on the 1st and finishes on the 14th (2-week slot) and I am listed as the 3rd trial.

OK, so things have just got real, I have a trial date. I was so anxious; my mind was constantly thinking up ways in which the next few months would pan out. I was also feeling relieved, I felt like I had been dangling off the edge of a building, hanging on only by the tips of my fingers for so long and didn't know how much longer I could do it, I just needed this trial to be over with. It's holding me hostage, unable to move forward and unable to get closure. I certainly had a renewed sense of hope.

I was advised by the DPP that I was trial number three. Which meant that my trial would only start after trial one and trial two were finished and if they took longer than expected we may not have time for trial three at all in the November sitting. This would mean a new trial date in 2021 something I couldn't even contemplate.

4th September

I received in the mail a 'Notice to Prospective Juror' from the Sheriff of Queensland requesting me for Jury Service for a two week period commencing 1st November. Yes, you are correct, that is the trial date for my case. Now I know this is an automated program but seriously with today's technology a small modification could certainly be made to ensure a jury notice is NEVER EVER sent to a victim relating to their own trial. It wasn't a massive deal, but it was just another thing, another thing I had to address, I had to respond, I had to explain. More rehashing the trauma. No victims awaiting trial should be called for any type of jury service in any court relating to a serious crime.

My Tribe Update – Seriously what are the chances of this happening????

I received a letter yesterday from the courts requesting me for 'Jury Duty' for two weeks from 1st Nov! Yes, that's my trial date.

Surely with technology today a search can be done on the name of the victim and perpetrator. Another obstacle I need to address for what seems ridiculous, insensitive, and unprofessional.
8 weeks to go

I wrote a letter to the Deputy Principal Registrar and Sheriff of Queensland Brisbane Supreme and District Courts. My letter explained my situation and I highlighted that this was yet another problem with our court system which re-traumatises victims over and over. I reminded her that I have been waiting three years for a trial which has been extremely difficult and now I had to fill in a form telling the court why I can't do jury duty for my own trial.

The registrar sincerely apologised for any distress caused. She assured me that it was a complete coincidence and was not intended to be insensitive. She stated that the system used to select potential jurors was indeed very old and that trying to get it to exclude victims was impossible. She asked if she could address the issue personally with the local court and assured me that I wasn't required to do anything further. The registrar was professional, polite and empathic and I thanked her for her quick reply.

Recommendation 8 – Jury Selection procedure updated

Scrap the current program used to select potential jurors for jury duty and implement an up to date, trauma informed program that is able to exclude victims of serious crimes to prevent further trauma.

2020 Third year waiting for trial

Leading up to trial I had to think about how I wanted to give evidence. It is now standard practice for the courtroom to be closed when victims of sexual crimes give evidence. This means no one from the public is allowed in the courtroom while I give evidence. This is a great step in the right direction, it means victims don't have to go into the personal intimate details for everyone to hear. It appears, the courts recognise on some level the difficulty victims have going to court, talking about the crimes and also simply seeing their perpetrator in court and how intimidating and frightening this is, so they do give you some options which are still required to be approved by the judge.

- You can be in a separate room and give evidence via live video.
- You can give your evidence in the courtroom but have a privacy screen up so that you don't actually have to see the perpetrator.
- You can select to have a support person with you in the court, sitting with you.

2nd October

My Tribe Update – four weeks until the trial.
I recently finished writing my victim impact statement which will be read before sentencing <u>only if he is convicted</u>. This was so difficult to write, I guess I have tried to minimise the impact it has had on me. Writing the statement forced me to look at the whole picture, to look at all aspects of my life and document it, all together. It's difficult to read and extremely sad but I feel I have articulated myself clearly and covered everything. So relieved that it's done now.
I still have a few decisions to make on how I give evidence. I have chosen my good friend Lesley to be my support person on the stand.

I can also request to give evidence from a separate room on video or to have a screen up in the court room so I can't see him. Ideally, I'd like to not have anything and look him straight in the eye but I'm just not sure if I'll be able to. Anyway, I have time to think about it. The DPP have reminded me to be prepared for it not to go ahead. I am the 3rd trial in the 2-week sitting, if one and two take longer than expected they won't have time for mine. Not too sure how I'll cope if that happens as it will move it to March/April next year. Anyway, fingers crossed it all goes ahead in November.

I have always said I wanted to be in the courtroom, I wanted the perpetrator to see me and I wanted to see him, to look him in the eyes. However, I did request permission for a support person. Selecting a person as a support was difficult, it needed to be someone who is able to hear the horrors of the story and remain neutral, to see me distressed and remain neutral and to be able to process the details without impacting their own mental health. It most certainly couldn't be family as it's just too close to home and would just be too much. I knew I only had two options. Option one- Kate who was also a witness for my case as she was required to give a statement and appear as a witness, so she was ruled out. Option two - my dear Scottish friend Lesley who I met at university, she is intelligent, calm and a highly skilled psychotherapist, she has the tools and experience, she was perfect. Lesley absolutely agreed to be my support person without hesitation.

17th October

My Tribe Update – Two weeks to trial. DPP called last week to advise that I have been bumped from 3rd trial to 4th. They reminded me to prepare for the possibility of there not being enough time for my trial to be heard and that it might be next year. I am staying positive and hopeful that my trial will be heard in November. At the moment, I can't even entertain the idea that it will be next year.

22nd October

My Tribe Post -1 week to court and we are now dealing with this... My 15-year-old daughter who is tiny, 40 kg and 5'1 was 'allegedly' physically hunted down and assaulted by two girls at a public school, girls twice her size, while bystanders cheered it on. Her best friend, who is smaller than her was forced into a physical fight and assaulted. While being physically assaulted, they were surrounded by 30 to 40 students cheering the offenders on saying 'smash her' 'take her to the ground' 'don't let her go' while multiple students filmed it all. It took three male teachers to get the offenders off. Early on, my daughter had asked a student leader for help who said, 'nah not getting involved.' She also approached someone she thought was a friend who told her to 'go away, I want nothing to do with it'. My daughter and her friend were the 'new' kids, having only been at the school for eight weeks. Luckily both girls are only bruised and sore, it could have been so much worse. We are absolutely disgusted and horrified, the videos are difficult to watch. All because apparently someone called someone a name..... It would appear that, bashing someone for name calling is standard practice here, with physical assaults almost daily. The school is run by delinquent children and needs to be closed down or to employ security guards.

One week until court and I am busy at home with a distraught teenager, appointments with doctor's, police, the school, and the education department. My daughter was unable to return to that school, both of the juvenile offenders, who had done this over and over to other students were issued a warning from police and expelled from school. We are also juggling numerous psychologist appointments for our other three teenagers, who are all struggling with their own mental health issues. It's a chaotic and stressful time.

3rd November

My Tribe Update – Trial #1 started as planned yesterday. My case is being mentioned tomorrow, a decision will then be made if I'm heard next week or next year.

4th November

My Tribe Court Update – I was just advised by the DPP my trial is now scheduled for the 9th of May 2021. Absolutely devastated.

6th November

I lodged a complaint with the DPP and emailed MP Shannon Fentiman who is the QLD Attorney General and Minister of Justice, The Minister for Women and The Minister for the Prevention of Domestic and Family Violence.

The DPP's response to my complaint was vague and basically stated that this is the process, things change all the time, often at short notice etc. etc.

Below is the response that I wrote out at the time but never sent as I was worried that I would be tarred as the problem case, the whinger, the case no one wants and the lady who rings up all the time. I was worried I would be allocated the youngest and least experienced public prosecutor.

2020 Third year waiting for trial

24th November 2020
Practice Manager
Office of Director of Public Prosecutions

Unfortunately, your repeated reassurance that the DPP and the courts make it a priority to finalise serious sexual assaults as soon as practicable does not provide me much comfort as this has not been my experience.

I know that the second week of the November sitting did not occur as I described in your email, no trial occurred during the second week of the sitting, why didn't my trial go ahead in the second week? Our regional courts can't afford to have a full week thrown away when we only sit every second month and not over December and January. It was the end of week one when it appeared trial two was not going ahead. From my point of view this left Monday to Thursday free for trial. One hearing on the Friday of the second week meant mine didn't go ahead... that is absurd.

It would appear the DPP is not willing to take any accountability for the delays in my case or professionalism of its legal staff. We can continue to go back and forth but it appears pointless.

There are still unanswered questions from my first email. I can only assume the DPP believes their system is running as good as possible and that there is no need to review procedures, question the process, review staffing or even pass my complaint onto a best practice committee as none of these options were mentioned in your reply. It was simply full of excuses.

I was speaking up not only for myself and my case but all the other victims in regional communities who have had to wait years to get to trial. The victims who unfortunately are unable to wait years and suicide before their trial and the marginalised and disadvantaged victims who are unable to speak up. Which now appears pointless.

I am extremely disappointed in the reply to my complaint from the DPP and only hope that my case is not impacted by this and that going forward I am treated in the victim centric trauma informed framework spoke about on your website which I am yet to see.

Trish Wyatt

11th November

My Tribe Update- So my complaint to the DPP is being looked at, they are mentioning it today to try to get trial #2 in the Jan sitting. Out of curiosity I checked the court lists for this week and trial #2 didn't proceed. There is no trial in my local court taking place this week. This hurts, being #3 I should have got that spot, but unfortunately, I was delisted last Thursday when I was allocated the May date. So, when trial two didn't occur the DPP did nothing to try to get me that spot, what a waste of a week considering we only get two weeks every second month. I'm starting to wonder if it's my case.... is it not strong enough? Is it because conviction rates are so low for rape and sexual violence? Is it an un-winnable case?

11th November

My Tribe Update Post – New court date is now 21st March 2021 as #1 trial.
Small win, only because I lodged a complaint. four months to wait is better than six months.

2020 Third year waiting for trial

At this point I found myself thinking a lot about all the other victims, the ones who were unable to articulate a complaint letter or advocate for themselves. The ones who didn't have the confidence to question our government and the ones too frightened to rock the boat. Who helps them during this process, who hears them, who even sees them? A process where victims have absolutely zero control over what's happening and yet, are expected to trust the powers that be! Trust that they are in fact doing the right thing, following procedures, and being treated as per the Charter of Victim Rights.

I also understand that for me to get number one trial in March meant that someone else's trial had to be pushed back and for that I am sorry. I am sorry your case was delayed to make room for mine. I am sorry that you too have probably waited years for your trial in our cruel system.

16th November

My Tribe Update – After wallowing in despair and anger the past two weeks, I have a renewed sense of optimism since writing this piece. It was very cathartic and powerful for my healing.

Trigger warning as this includes some details of the assault which some may find confronting.

The woman in the corner
There is a woman in the corner of the room sitting on the floor, trying to be as small as possible, with her arms wrapped around her knees as she watches what unfolds.

A woman is lying naked on a bed.

Don't Report Rape

A man also naked is climbing on top of her body, he kneels on her chest, the full weight of his body on her chest. He shuffles on his knees up towards her face, with each knee pinning her shoulders down, the woman sinks into the mattress. He forces himself into her mouth, the woman is struggling to breathe, with the weight of the man on her, her nostrils become blocked by the man's body. Struggling to breathe, she tries opening her mouth as wide as she can to get some air while he thrusts aggressively. The man doesn't say a word. The woman does not speak, her physical attempts to resist seem to result in him being more forceful. She is frozen in fear, a vacant blank look on her face.

He climbs off her body and begins to rape her, her body is still almost lifeless. While doing this he puts both hands around her neck and strangles her. She is squirming, her legs are kicking, she wonders if he is going to kill her. She wonders how long it takes to die from this. Her face turns red; he releases his hands from her throat. She gasps for air and tries to take some breaths. While she is getting her breath back he moves one arm back, so his hand is pointed at the ceiling then swings with full force, slapping her across her face. Her head swings hard from one side to the other. Tears begin running down her face. She looks confused..... this is not what she expected.

She lost count of how many times he strangled her, how many times he hit her and how many times he raped her; throwing her around like a rag doll, she is helpless. This cycle of sexual violence continues for the next eight hours, over and over.

A one point the woman watching thought she was going to witness a murder, *another woman lost at the hands of a violent man she thought*, another statistic.

The man has the woman in a choke hold from behind, she cannot move, and it appears that the slightest move on his part would snap her neck.

2020 Third year waiting for trial

Did she have children? Would she see them again? How many other women has he done this to? How will she escape this?

At some point the woman watching merged with the woman in the bed.

Confused and disorientated she slowly and quietly creeps out of the bed while he is asleep, grabs her belongings, exits the room and rushes to her car.

I was the woman in the corner.

I survived because I left my body, I survived because of the woman in the corner.

My physical body may not have died that night but a part of me did. I continue to grieve the loss of who I was before the assault. The happy, funny, easy going and patient Trish no longer exists, and I miss her so much.

As a result of the assault, I suffer from complex PTSD, anxiety and depression leaving me unable to work in my trained profession as a social worker or in fact hold a job at all. Financially I am now dependent on the disability pension.

While I continue to heal and discover the new me, I am hopeful to reinvent myself to an even better version of the old me. A version of me who is stronger, a woman who advocates against sexual violence, a woman who can speak for those who can't.

It's been almost three years since the assault and my long-awaited trial is set for March 2021. I am determined to turn my trauma into purpose by fiercely addressing the ways in which our laws and systems further traumatise victims, making it extremely hard to report these types of crimes.

Just to add to the shit that I am dealing with, Just when you think that nothing else can go wrong. I find a lump in my breast. Doctor's appointments, scans, a biopsy and the constant thought – do I have breast cancer now?

24th December

I received correspondence in response to my complaint to the Attorney-General from the Acting Chief of Staff to the Hon. Shannon Fentiman MP, Attorney-General. She stated that Shannon Fentiman asked the acting chief of staff to respond on Ms Fentiman's behalf. In her response she acknowledged the seriousness of the crimes, the trauma and impact these crimes have had on my life and my disappointment regarding the delay in finalising prosecution. It was certainly nice to feel heard and validated. She assured me that the DPP takes all sexual offending seriously with protocols and procedures in place to ensure victims are treated as per the Charter of Victim Rights under the Victims of Crime Assistance Act 2009 and assured me that matters of this serious nature get priority when listing. She also assured me that all staff at the DPP have received appropriate information about trauma awareness. She went through my case, explaining each step and why it was delayed, not everything rang true, and I am still unsure as to why my trial was not heard during the second week of the November sitting.

Property Settlement with my ex-husband is still dragging on. My eldest two children still only maintain a very distant relationship with their father and continue accessing support for their mental health.

Chapter 10

2021 Trial Prep

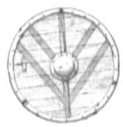

5th January

It was an intense Christmas and New Year period, unfortunately due to the public holidays I didn't get my breast biopsy results back until the new year. Thankfully the lump was benign. Phew, thank fucking god!

11th January

My Tribe Update – three years today. . .10 weeks until court – '' –

17th February

My Tribe Update – So it's four weeks to trial, I need to start preparing for court. If anyone has any tips or suggestions, please let me know. As far as I'm aware, I will only get DPP support on the day of trial or possibly the day before.

At this point in time, I have not had any conversations with the prosecutor and have no idea what the case looks like, what evidence they have used or not used... nothing. I am told that on Monday 22nd I will meet the crown prosecutor and walk through the court room. The jury would also be selected on the Monday. Tuesday at 9 a.m. the trial will commence. I have not seen or spoken to the detective in approximately two or more years, when he issued me the subpoenas. I was assigned a police officer from the Vulnerable Persons Unit immediately following the assault and assured they, together with the detective would remain in contact and provide support up to the trial however apart from a few phone calls immediately following the assault, I had not heard from the Vulnerable Persons Unit officer either. I had no one to advise what to wear to court or what to expect. The first time I receive any of this information is the day before the trial. I relied on what I knew about the courts from TV shows and by googling 'what to wear to court'. Googles advice was smart business wear, long sleeved, dark plain colours no patterns or bright colours.

27th February

My Tribe Update – three weeks until court.
If anyone would like to attend court, I'd love the support.

2021 Trial Prep

The courtroom will be closed when I give evidence but will be open for the public the rest of the trial. Don't wear any of our activists' shirts as I'm pretty sure they aren't allowed in the courtroom.

I am starting to familiarise myself with my statement and I'm going to start reading my victim impact statement out aloud for practice as I'd like to read it in court when and if he is convicted.

I'm looking for volunteers willing to hear me read my victim impact statement, maybe through a group zoom. This doesn't include details of the crimes, just how the crimes have impacted my life. Let me know if you are interested.

Providing all goes to plan.

Mon 21st March – most likely jury selection

Tue 22nd March - trial commences, I give evidence, may finish the same day. If not, it will finish Wednesday 23rd.

3rd March

I read my Victim Impact Statement out loud to the Tribe Members who were able to make the zoom call. As difficult as it was to read out, I was feeling good, I felt like I had covered everything and felt confident that I would be able to read it myself and not have someone read it for me.

Messages between Kate and I, the day before court.

Kate – How are you feeling

Trish – OK, trying to stay grounded. Really anxious, nauseous and want it over

Kate – Yeah. Just remember you have done nothing wrong. This process is about justice for you, holding him accountable and keeping others safe. Stay strong, you can do this, replace those anxious voices with positive ones xx

Trish – Thank you, how are you feeling?

Kate – Same as you but probably not to the same extent. It's an awful feeling knowing that his defense is going to use me and try to make a liar out of my friend.

Trish – we got this xx

Kate – Yes we do!!

21st March

My dear friend Lesley who was my court support person, arrived at my place on Monday morning 21st March. Together with Jamie and I, we met the crown prosecutor at the courthouse Monday afternoon. The crown prosecutor introduced herself, and to be honest when I first saw her I thought how much she looked like Elle, Reece Witherspoon's character from Legally Blonde, she was young, attractive, blonde, tiny and had a great collection of pumps in her office. She advised us who the allocated judge for the trial was and stated that he is lovely.

The crown prosecutor asked the bailiff to walk us through the courtroom to help reduce anxiety which was well worthwhile. I was shown where everyone sits, where the offender sits and where I sit. It was explained again that I can choose how I give evidence i.e., in another room, with a privacy screen up or with a support person. I advised the crown prosecutor that I have decided to give my evidence in the courtroom with a support person. The crown prosecutor commented on how brave my choice was and that a lot of witnesses are unable to do it. She told me that she would advise the judge of my decision and request permission for me to have a support person. The crown prosecutor asked if anyone had advised me on the court proceedings and what to expect, I said no. She went on to explain that the defence barrister would put forward suggestions and that I am to agree or disagree with the suggestions made. Her advice to me was to just be honest, take my time, ask for the question to be repeated if necessary and just answer honestly.

It was at this point that the crown prosecutor advised me that she was considering dropping one of the charges as she didn't feel she had enough evidence to prove it. The charge she wanted to drop was Assault Occasioning Bodily Harm which mainly related to the bruising on my neck from being strangled multiple times over the evening. She stated that she really needed to be able to prove a specific incident caused the harm and as there were so many incidents of strangulation, she didn't think she could link it to a specific one. Sounds crazy right? You might need to read that sentence again. This charge was also the only charge that was linked to physical evidence which was the doctor's report from the hospital. She told me she would think more about it tonight and decide in the morning. I wasn't really sure what this meant, again I trusted in the system, and I guess with eight charges, dropping one still meant seven, and remember we only need guilty on one right?

The crown prosecutor advised us who the defence barrister representing the defendant was and that she was from the Aboriginal and Torres Strait Islander Legal Service. The crown prosecutor told us she was actually a bit star struck by the defence barrister, as she saw her as a mentor, someone she looked up to professionally and that they had previously worked together. The defence prosecutor was a highly experience and respected barrister. So, already I am sensing a slight imbalance in prosecutors, solely based on age and experience. However, I have faith in the system and the three of us all had a good feeling with the crown prosecutor, despite her youthful age, she presented as confident and feisty, we affectionately referred to her as our pocket rocket.

The crown prosecutor showed us the area and room where we can gather and wait tomorrow. She asked us to come in a little earlier in the morning so she could do some roleplay with me on the types of suggestions and questions the prosecution would make to me, again to help reduce anxiety. We said our goodbyes and told her we would see her in the morning.

21st March

My Tribe Update – Summary of today

Met with prosecutor, went through my statement, reviewed the charges, and looked in the court room

*Jury is being selected tomorrow morning at 10

* I am first to give evidence and will take all day Tuesday, closed court (not open to public)

*Wednesday the rest of the witnesses are called in open court (open to the public)

*Verdict Wed afternoon or Thursday

22nd March

My Tribe Update – Feeling strong this morning ladies, all ready with my teal blouse and teal hair wrap. The colour teal is the official and recognised colour for Sexual Violence awareness and the reason I chose to wear teal every day at court.

I'm drawing on my female ancestors today by wearing my Nannas Virgo pendant and my Great Aunt Freda's broach. Got my essential oils on, my spinning ring and blue tac to fidget with. Thank you everyone for the well wishes, love and strength. I got this!

8:00 a.m. We head into the local District Court.

Chapter 11

Trial Day One: Morning Session

I nervously walk up the entry steps holding Jamie's hand and enter the Court House. After going through security, we walk upstairs where the courtroom is and sit in the waiting room we were shown yesterday.

In the room with me, Jamie and Lesley are my parents, my sister and her husband, my brother and his wife. I also had about eight friends who attended at various times over the three days. The room we waited in was not big enough for everyone, so my support spilled out into the public waiting area.

Not long after arriving, the crown prosecutor called us into her office. She asked if I had any questions, advised me that I will be called as the first witness. She stated that she had decided to drop the Assault Occasioning Bodily Harm Charge as she felt the case was stronger without it. She advised me that a jury of twelve had been selected (with two reserve jurors in case Covid prevented one of the twelve from appearing) and while she was able to make some swaps, she was disappointed with the average age of the jurors being elderly and male. A lot of regional communities typically attract older Australians and retirees. Regional jury panels like mine, lack the diversity that city juries have based purely on where we live. Is this fair or unfair? Are the world views of retired Australians the same as a 20 or 30 year old Australian? Should it be that all ages are covered when selecting a jury? How about the male to female ratio? Should it be as 50/50 as possible? What if it was a jury full of women or full of men? Would that be just? Would that be fair?

Tuesday 22nd March

Day 1

During the following three days, I remain outside the courtroom in the waiting room. It was recommended by the crown prosecutor that I do not sit in the public courtroom gallery just in case we needed a re-trial. Therefore, the only time I entered the courtroom was as a witness to give evidence and when the verdict was read. To understand exactly what occurred in the courtroom, I am reading through the official transcripts. As I write, it's literally the first time I am reading them, it's extremely traumatic and confronting.

While waiting for court to commence we could hear someone whaling and sobbing within the courthouse, but we weren't sure where it was coming from.

Trial Day One: Morning Session

The crown prosecutor advised us that the offender was hyperventilating and sobbing in distress, poor fella, guess he knew that these should have been his last days of freedom. She was concerned as she was worried that if he was unable to pull himself together, the judge may rule a mistrial and the courts would be required to allocate another court date in the future. So, already I am thinking - *oh my god, here we go again, all prepared for trial, and it may not go ahead.*

10:31 a.m. – The judge opened the court, both prosecutors introduced themselves. Before the trial started there were a few issues that the judge needed to address.

The crown prosecutor advised the judge about the removal of the 8th charge of Assault Occasioning Bodily Harm and amended the indictment from eight charges to seven, which were.

Count	Official Charge	Referred to in court as…
Count 1	Rape	Oral
Count 2	Rape	Vaginal
Count 3	Common Assault	Slapping
Count 4	Rape	Anal
Count 5	Rape	Vaginal
Count 6	Attempted Rape	Fisting
Count 7	Rape	Anal

It would appear that the stretching incident, digging his elbow into my chest repeatedly and dragging it across my chest to cause pain, smothering my face forcefully with his hands, putting me in a frightening choke hold and multiple strangulation incidents <u>didn't attract any criminal charge at all,</u> or were perhaps just lumped into the rape charges. Does that sound fair and just? How are offenders held accountable for these acts of violence, and not just violence during a sexual act?

Recommendation 9 – Laws specific to sexual violence

We need crimes specific to sexual violence, right now our system only takes into account rape, which is penetration without consent. I believe there should also be rape with violence laws to cover these violent acts of sexual violence. There is a big difference from being raped which is horrific enough, let alone being raped and physically assaulted at the same time particularly to the point that you may actually die. Sexual violence as defined by Queensland Government website is 'Sexual Violence (including sexual abuse and assault) is any unwanted sexual behaviour towards another person'. Personally, I don't think this is good enough.

With Rough sex becoming more 'normal' as seen in porn, tv shows and movies. It needs to be defined within the law. Rough Sex can be split into two categories. Mild and playful rough sex includes spanking and hair pulling while violent rough sex includes slapping, strangulation, fisting and suffocation. Consent for rough sex must be gained through an affirmative consent model and must include an agreement on a safe word, in which either party can use to stop all interactions immediately.

Sexual violence as defined by Queensland Government website: Sexual Violence (including sexual abuse and assault) is any unwanted sexual behaviour towards another person. Types of sexual violence include:

<u>Sexual Assault</u> – includes rape and attempted rape as well as unwanted sexual touching. It also states consent should be given

Trial Day One: Morning Session

freely and voluntarily. It also states that consent <u>CAN NOT BE GIVEN</u> if you are:

   a) forced, threatened, or intimidated – applicable in my case
   b) unconscious or asleep – applicable in my case
   c) are under the influence of alcohol – applicable in my case
   d) misled in anyway e.g., someone pretending to be a doctor – not applicable in my case
   e) under the age of 16 years old – not applicable in my case

<u>Sexual Harassment</u> – any form of unwanted and unwelcomed sexual attention which includes suggestive comments, staring, displaying sexually offensive material, requesting sex or other favours. This type of sexual violence was not applicable in my case.

<u>Image based abuse</u> – when someone takes or shares a nude or sexual image of people without their permission. This type of sexual violence was not applicable in my case.

That is it.

The judge asked the defendant to stand while he read out each of the seven charges. The defendant was asked how he pleads to each charge to which the defendant responded 'not guilty' to all seven charges.

The jury was empanelled which basically means the judge clearly outlines their role as a juror and that it was the responsibility of the jury and the jury only to determine guilt or not. The judge explained that his role in the proceedings was to ensure that the trial is conducted according to the law. He also highlighted that the defendant is not required to prove his innocence, and that it's the prosecutor's job to prove to the jury beyond a reasonable doubt the defendant's guilt based on the evidence presented.

The jury was retired for lunch to allow the judge to address some matters with the defendant's barrister, who made an application to the judge with relation to Section 4 of the Criminal Law (sexual offences) Act. The defence barrister stated that this act is to prevent the complainant (me) from being cross examined about any aspect of promiscuity - chastity as it is named in the act.

Subsection 1 of the act states that.

The court shall not receive evidence of and shall disallow any questions as to the general reputation of the complainant with respect to chastity

This law is in place to prevent slut shaming.

The act continues:

Without leave of the court, cross-examination should not be permitted as to the sexual activities of the complainant with any person; and evidence shall not be received as to the sexual activities of the complainant with any person.

Fairly clear right? According to the law, the defence is not allowed to ask me questions of sexual relations or activity with other men. Here is the loophole 'unless leave (aka permission) is granted', so if the defence barrister can convince the judge that her questions are within the law, that she would do so delicately and not in an underhanded way of getting evidence of promiscuity in front of a jury, she will be given permission to do so. The defence barrister was requesting permission to cross examine me on three issues:

Trial Day One: Morning Session

1. Permission to ask me whether I had sex with another man the night before the night of the incident which she stated was NOT contested by the crown prosecutor. The defence barrister claimed this relevant because in my statement I do acknowledge stating that I had sex recently and implied that the bruising I presented with in emergency on the Monday may have been from that person and not from the defendant as I allege. The nature of the injuries I presented with mainly consisted of neck bruising. I don't know about you, but I don't believe an injury of bruising to the neck is a common injury for standard consensual sex. Was she implying strangulation forceful enough to leave bruising, may be something I regularly participated in? Because, if this was investigated the crown prosecutor could have called the person I did have consensual sex with the night or two before the assault, he could have been called as a witness. He would have verified that strangulation was not something we had ever done or even spoken about and that it would have absolutely been impossible for him to inflict those injuries. He could have also verified the type of relationship we had, we were both out of long-term marriages, single and found comfort with each other. He could have also verified that I spoke to him about the assault a few days after. This opportunity was missed, this person was not called as a witness.

2. The defence barrister requested permission to ask me if I had ever participated in anal sex or fisting, not leading up to the incident but ever. She stated that because these two acts are part of the offences she wanted to determine if I regularly took part in these activities or not. Claiming that if I did regularly participate in these acts consensually

in the past that it puts a different spin on the offending of that night. So, if I had ever participated in anal sex or fisting in the past, then consent is questionable? Then it's not rape? That's outrageous. What I have or haven't done sexually with other partners is completely irrelevant, it has absolutely nothing to do with the incident with the offender, nothing. The defence barrister assured the judge that her request was not to be judgemental towards me and what sexual conduct I chose to engage in, it was purely to provide a more balanced context for the jury on these two acts.

OK, so going off this theory if the crimes include anal sex, you can ask about the victim's history of anal sex because one of the rapes relate to anal sex. So, does this mean for vaginal rapes, the defence is allowed to ask the witness about her history of vaginal sex? I doubt it. Should I have been asked about my oral sex history as well, seen as though one of the rape charges relates to oral sex? Of course not. In my opinion this request is purely to put evidence of promiscuity and discredit my reputation in front of the elderly jury.

3. As they had all my text messages from when I handed my phone over innocently at the police station over three years ago. The assault occurred on Friday 11th Jan, the defence barrister found a text I sent to a man in which I said 'Hey Handsome xxx' on Saturday 12th Jan. She claimed that she didn't believe someone who had been violently raped the night before would initiate this type of text with another man, and that the jury should be made aware of this.

Firstly, I would like to know what expertise the defence barrister has on how exactly a person is supposed to respond after being

Trial Day One: Morning Session

violently raped. Does she have qualifications in psychology and trauma that I am unaware of. Clearly there must be a right and wrong way to respond, right? This too is absurd. Isn't this what happened to Lindy Chamberlain? She didn't respond the way the public expected her to respond if a dingo did in fact take her baby. So, she was jailed for the murder of her child, that was over forty years ago. Anyone who has the slightest training in trauma knows that it is a very complex and individual experience. It often takes days and even weeks for the reality of the situation to actually sink in for a victim.

As I stated in my statement, initially I wasn't even sure a crime had been committed which was why I went to QPS on Sunday to get advice. The man I texted was a sweet man I had been chatting with who has extremely low confidence and self-esteem with women. He lived a long way away, was never considered a potential partner, we were friends. The defence barrister went on to explain to the judge that the rest of the messages she read were all standard chit chat you would expect on a dating site, she stated she never saw any messages stating, 'lovely to get your message but I'm taking a break from dating' or 'I need time with my kids'. She said there was no sense of stepping away from her involvement in the dating site. Again, I guess that is the expected response of someone who was violently raped, and again, what trauma expert or evidence supports her theory?

The judge asked what the crown's position was on these three requests. The crown prosecutor stated that she has no issue with the defence raising the first matter with me. Remember that was about asking me about my sexual history with regards to anal and fisting. I am not sure why the crown was happy for the defence to cross examine me on this. I still don't know the answer to this. Due to the crown's position on this the judge granted permission for the defence barrister to cross examine me on this. She was given permission to slut shame me on the stand.

The crown did attempt to object to the other two issues by stating that it is indeed going too far and that it does paint a picture of the complainant (me) in a certain way in front of the jury, particularly with relation to the third, talking to other men. The judge stated that he too questioned the third issue whether it should be granted, but then he referred the crown prosecutor to section 5,

Evidence relating to or tending to establish the fact that a complainant has engaged in sexual activity with a person or persons is not a proper matter for cross examination as to credit unless, because of special circumstances, the court considers the evidence would be likely to materially impair confidence in reliability of the complainant's evidence.

The judge stated that it has the potential to impair confidence in the reliability of my evidence if I was seeking contact with others shortly after the alleged offending.

Remember we are talking about a text that said 'Hi Handsome' that's it, no evidence of trying to meet up or anything.

The Judge granted permission to the defence to cross examine me on all three issues. Part of his reason for this decision was because she indicated that she would do it as delicately as possible, with a warning from the judge not to overstep the mark.

Let's see how 'delicately' the defence is able to raise these topics with me when I am on the stand.

Trial Day One: Morning Session

Recommendation 10 – Ban slut shaming in our courtrooms

No surprise here. It's clearly quite easy for defence prosecutors to obtain permission from a judge to slut shame a victim on the stand during cross examination. The criminal law act (sexual offences) Act clearly needs re-writing. What is the point of having a law to prevent slut shaming and victim blaming if prosecutors can still ask permission to do it under special circumstances?

The crown then discussed with the judge my request for a support person while I give evidence. The judge had no issue with my request and even stated he would arrange for a chair to be placed next to mine in the court room. That is until the defence objected to my request by stating to the judge, that she did have an issue with my request as I was clearly an adult.

My only assumption here is that the defence is implying I am a big girl and can sit in the big courtroom on my own like an adult. Thankfully the judge addressed this insensitive and inappropriate comment and stated that my request is in fact common and routine and typically used in matters like this. The defence barrister's argument was with regards to line of sight and claiming my support person may influence the jury and she suggested the public gallery a more appropriate place for my support person to sit. However again the judge explained the fact that the courtroom will be empty of only the required people and that, the judge clearly approved a support person to be seated within close proximity to me, to which the crown agreed and acknowledged.

Don't Report Rape

The final issue raised this morning was when the bailiff handed the judge a piece of paper that stated that three of the jurors knew each other. Two jurors currently worked together and another juror previously worked with them. Is this a problem?

The judge stated that he didn't see it as an issue and that they are all to do their job impartially.

The morning session was adjourned at 12:02 p.m. and was due to return at 1:01 p.m.

Chapter 12

Trial Day One: Afternoon Session

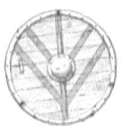

Now, it's really important for me to remind you all that at this point, I have no idea at all what has been discussed with the Judge. Nothing at all. I had family and friends in the gallery, but they were not allowed to discuss anything at all with me. Again, this was the advice we received from the crown, in case of a mistrial.

Before court resumed the crown prosecutor called me into her office. She told me that permission was granted by the judge for Lesley to sit near me in the courtroom while I give evidence. She said they weren't sure yet exactly where her chair will be situated but she would work it out. Lesley was given strict instructions on what she was not allowed to do in the courtroom; no eyerolling, no raising eyebrows, no emotion, no sighs, basically sit like a statue to ensure she doesn't influence the jury in any way.

The crown prosecutor also told me that the defence barrister had been given leave on something, but she wasn't allowed to tell me what it was. Understandably confused, I asked what even is 'leave'? I didn't even know what this phrase meant. The crown said that it's basically permission to ask you questions on certain topics, but apologetically stated she can't say anymore. Horrified and stunned, this is within minutes of me being called to the stand. I knew they had all the messages from my phone, and I suspected it may have to do with my casual relationship with another man. I had not seen the messages or evidence they had on this, even though it came from my phone. The crown prosecutor could see the distress on my face and advised me to just be honest and I'll be fine, just be honest.

I had no one present who could explain any of this to me. I was about to go on the stand, we hadn't had time to role play any scenarios with the crown as planned, I don't even know what I am expected to do in the courtroom, am I allowed to look at the jury, the judge, what sort of things can I say? I was absolutely petrified.

1:02 Court resumes

The crown prosecutor made her opening statement where she summarised what happened that evening from my perspective, followed by a brief opening statement from the defence barrister. The judge closed the courtroom, and I was called in as the first witness to give evidence.

The crown prosecutor opened the door to the small waiting room we were sitting in and indicated it was time. I hugged my partner

Trial Day One: Afternoon Session

and family members through tears as they all gave positive words of encouragement. I grabbed Lesley's hand, took a deep breath and we entered the court room. As you enter the court room, standing at the entry door, straight ahead farthest away is the judge sitting at about twelve o'clock, then legal representatives in front of him and then approximately six or seven rows on both sides of the door for the public gallery. The witness box was located at three o'clock, to the far right of the room. The Jury sat in two rows facing the witness box, from eight o'clock to eleven o'clock. The defendant sits in a small glass room at seven o'clock.

Despite the judge approving Lesley to sit within close proximity to me, there was no chair for Lesley, she was led to the front row of the public gallery, which was approximately four metres away. Not at all what was discussed and agreed with the judge during the morning session. But again, there was no one representing me, no one looking out for my best interest, and just another reason why victims of sex crimes must have legal representation.

My whole body is shaking. I am trying to focus on my breathing as I walk into the court room and sit in the witness box. Let's talk about the witness box in my local district courtroom. A chair is placed inside a wooden box, when seated in the chair the wooden sides were as high as my chest/shoulders. There was a screen mounted to the left of the witness box which impaired my view to both my support person in the public gallery and the crown prosecutor. To see both people I was required to sit up tall and either lean forward or backwards, I had to poke my head around the screen to see them. The line of sight from the witness box - you can draw a straight line from me sitting in the witness box directly through the defence barrister and right behind her was the offender. So, when the defence was addressing me, whenever I looked at her, I could see the offender. There was actually no way for me to not see the offender when answering her. Mind you, he was able to slide to the right of his room and hide himself from my view, which he did.

> **Recommendation 11 –** Trauma informed courtrooms
>
> **My local Court was recently renovated surely a more trauma informed configuration of the courtroom could have been taken into account.**

The Crown prosecutor spent one hour going through the incident from how we first made contact to the details of the evening the assault took place. I have to say, my version of events was pretty spot on with my statement and my memory of recalling the evening. All the information was the same the only discrepancy was the order or sequence of events. Even when I wrote my statement over three years ago, I explained that I wasn't sure exactly the order of events, was this before that or did this happen after that. Several photos were presented on the screen on the witness box and when asked I drew a circle around the bruising on my neck as seen in the pictures. The pictures were not that great, but it was all we had, they were taken by me on my phone and as a person who doesn't bruise easily the bruises were not very dark. Unfortunately, QPS never asked to take any pictures of my injuries, so I took some myself. I was asked to demonstrate various actions e.g., how he strangled my neck, the way he struck me with his hands, the choke hold and a brief description of how he attempted to insert his fist and demonstrate how his hands were placed during the stretching incident. After one hour on the stand answering the crown prosecutor's questions, court was adjourned for fifteen minutes.

Trial Day One: Afternoon Session

2:49 p.m. I was called back into the closed courtroom to be cross examined by the defence. The judge welcomed Lesley and I back into the court room and reminded me that I could request a break at any time and stated that it was quite possible I would be required to return tomorrow to finalise my evidence.

The defence started by clarifying the lead up to the meeting. She asked me to confirm what alcohol I purchased, what he was drinking, how much he drank. I was asked if I had ever had anal sex with anyone ever and also if I had ever participated in fisting. Two questions she was given permission to ask me. What followed was a detailed argument over the definition of fisting. I am unsure why this was necessary ... does it matter if it was fingers, knuckles or a whole fist? She was alluding that the act wasn't actually fisting at all and claimed what I was describing was fingers inserted. I had to explain, actually it was four fingers and the thumb brought together to a point and inserted with pressure followed by a corkscrew action, to the point of feeling pain. Yes, I had to demonstrate this in the court room as well as answer how deep I thought his hand was inserted, multiple times.

Here is the thing, so much of this case is based on the order of things. For example:

The defence claimed I changed my story on the stand with regards to the order of events around the testing incident. She claimed that the testing incident as written in my statement occurred before the consensual sex. My statement does not say that and in fact mentions multiple times that I am unsure of the order. Her point being that if he had tried to grab my throat first, why would I then have consensual sex with him. I tried to clarify the details stating that because it was three years ago, over three years ago and it's been a traumatic three years for me and I'm trying to recall something that happened multiple times down to one little instance that I might have switched around the wrong way.

I tried to explain multiple times how hard I found it to recall the exact order of events or how many times certain acts occurred. I said things like; I can't remember half of it anyway; I'd be woken up by a slap to the face or someone penetrating me. I, I don't know how many times it was. I said it was a number of times– a large number of sexual interactions occurred over an eight-hour period, an eight-hour period. And I'm trying to think which one came first ... I've had two bottles of wine; I've had marijuana which I haven't had since I was a teenager and I'm trying to remember events from three years ago and the order they went in?

The defence went on, letting the jury know who I spoke with on the Saturday after the assault. Highlighting messages to my mum and to my friend Justine that do not indicate that I had been assaulted. I guess that is another expected response, that a victim runs and tells everyone what happened straight away. In my case and for many victims, the devasting reality had not even sunk in yet. She then pointed out that I messaged the man I had been seeing on Saturday saying, 'Hi Handsome', this was the term I always used when chatting with him. Again, I am not sure what the point of this was other than to slut shame me. I believe she was implying that If I was in fact assaulted the way I described I would not have sent him that text, so, I must not have been assaulted. Same with a text I sent to another friend saying, 'Hi it's Trish'. This text was used to imply to the jury that I was already setting up more dates, so if I was already on the hunt for my next conquest the assault could not have happened right? These messages were taken off my phone without legal advice and were now being used against me.

Trial Day One: Afternoon Session

She went on talking about how I reported to police and when I met the detective at the hospital, and she stated.

Here is the kicker.... Ready

She actually asked me if I told the detective when I reported the crimes that in the three days prior that I had sex with three different men? And asked me if indeed the detective was aware of this.

Yep, it's completely allowed to just make up complete rubbish and present it as fact. What the fuck! Where has this come from? Have I missed something? This was a complete lie.

Horrified, I clarified that she had just stated three different men to which she replied quite matter of fact, yes.

I asked her to tell me who these three men were because I certainly didn't know who they were. I stated that there was only one other man beside the offender. The man I had been seeing casually.

The defence followed with an apology stating she made a mistake and was confused. She went on and clarified I sent another man a text on the Saturday.

I guess sending a text saying 'Hi, it's Trish,' also means I had sex with him on Saturday too.

So, you can make a completely false allegation so long as you follow it up with, 'oh sorry, I got that wrong'.

Whether I had sex with one other man or ten other men while trying to get a medical examination after an assault is completely irrelevant. My offender used condoms; the purpose of the examination was to document injuries obtained by an act of violence not to test fluid to see who I have had sex with. The defence claimed that she was trying to determine if the detective knew this information or not as it may have informed his decision on the type of examination I was subjected to. I call bull shit on this and believe she just wanted to paint a picture of my promiscuity which unfortunately she was given permission to do. At no point did the crown object to any of these questions or try to retract the comment the defence made about their being three different men. I was then forced to educate the defence on what it is actually like to try to get a medical examination after a rape for regional women. I explained that I didn't even get a proper examination because we don't have that service in our community. Women in regional communities don't get the same treatment as women in the city. I should have got a rape kit. I didn't. The person who does that (job) wasn't in the hospital that day. So, I just missed out. All that was done was a doctor physically looked over my body. That's it.

The defence did a great job getting confused particularly with the order of events and I have no doubt this was deliberate and after one hour thankfully the judge could see me struggling and called for a break.

As soon as I was out of the court, I ran toward my family and the first person I found was my good friend Angela who just put her arms out and caught me, I could barely stand. My family surrounded me, and I just sobbed and sobbed.

Pulling myself together as much as I could to re-enter the courtroom at 3:55 p.m. Again, we re-hash the order of things… so was that before the anal, then the slapping, then this then that… It went on and on.

Trial Day One: Afternoon Session

I end up saying, that the most detailed account of what happened is in my statement. It was done two days after. I'm – over three years. I'm having great difficulty. I feel like I am getting caught up in the details and it's very difficult for me to remember that long ago.

Literally as I am typing this I am shaking, feeling nauseous and I'm having to take a lot of breaks. I am struggling with emotions of sadness and anger. My Dad just called me and after telling him how difficult this is, he told me to make sure I document how hard this is and how difficult it is, write from your heart Trish, he said, people need to know.

The defence refers back to my statement confirming that the detective was patient and gave me ample opportunity to review and change things where I thought necessary. I told her that yes, the detective was very patient, and also horrified with what he was typing. What a shame the detective wasn't called as a witness to give evidence, the defence could have asked him herself. The detective sat in the waiting room for three days and was never called, but we will discuss that one later.

The defence asked if there was anything preventing me from leaving the motel room like a deadlock, highlighted that there was a police station not too far away, people in the room next door, moments when the perpetrator was asleep. All implying why I didn't leave.

I tried to explain why I was unable to leave how my body would not cooperate. She then highlighted the fact that I did describe myself pacing around the room in a small circle to which I replied that yes, that was the next day when I was sober.

After another half an hour on the stand, court was adjourned until 10 a.m. tomorrow.

22nd March

My Tribe Update -Tuesday's update

Jury was selected, opening statements made, I was first on the stand. Didn't get finished so I will be back on the stand tomorrow morning at 10, followed by the rest of the witnesses in open court.

I feel I went OK, locked eyes with the offender which was tough but then avoided looking at him. He had three support people that looked like his mother, father, and partner.

Open court Tomorrow should start about 11.

That evening I was sitting on my veranda having a glass of wine with Lesley and I saw a shooting star! Had to be a good sign, right?

Chapter 13

Trial Day Two: Morning Session

10:08 a.m. I returned to the witness box in the closed court room.

The defence continued to pull apart my statement suggesting that I had examined it overnight, identified flaws in my story and now want to change my version of events to fit the story I told yesterday. *What the actual fuck? What possible motive would I have to make this whole story up.* More of asking me about the order of events, not to clear things up for the jury but to confuse them, just as she was confusing me. For example:

'So, now your saying...'

'I thought you just said...'

Don't Report Rape

'Which is it?'

'You were expecting sexual intercourse weren't you...'

'Didn't you say yesterday...'

I stated that if I did indeed scour through my statement, I would be very clear on what happened, I am trying to give an honest account of what occurred.

I had just left a twenty year marriage, I was trying to get back into the dating world. Last time I dated, we didn't even have mobile phones. I'm on a dating app trying to get back into it, not really knowing how it worked. It's a completely different world out there now for dating.

After some heated back and forth the defence firmly instructed me to listen to her question and then I could answer it. She told me that if she was cutting me off the crown can object.

I am extremely distressed at this point, most of my evidence was given through sobbing breathlessness and now I have been told off by the defence barrister for misunderstanding her questions.

Important note: so far there has not been one single objection from the crown.

The actual wording in my statement she was referring to is that I stated I was prepared for the first encounter and had consented to one sexual encounter and that I was going to see how things progressed before consenting to any further encounters.

Trial Day Two: Morning Session

I confirmed that yes, I consent before every encounter, I think about am I going to do this, am I not going to do this, do I feel safe, do I not feel safe.

She then discussed my state of mind with regards to being there to hook up with the perpetrator, and that sex was on the cards.

I confirmed one hundred per cent that I went there for casual sex, but I didn't go there to be strangled, hit and suffocated.

She asked questions about the testing incident in the bathroom when he attempted to get consent to hit and strangle me. She claimed my statement said the testing occurred first followed by the consensual sex on the balcony and that overnight I realised this doesn't make sense, who would have consensual sex with someone after the testing incident.

I acknowledge that these details are confusing in my statement, how the whole night was confusing.

She then went on and suggested that I changed my story to make myself and my story look better.

I assured the courtroom that there is no way that if a man grabbed my throat and tried to strike me that I would participate in that. *I'm completely against violence, I'm a professional social worker... there is no way.*

The defence highlighted that I had every opportunity to make that clear to the police and that is the order you chose to put it in.

I replied yes I did have multiple opportunities to get my version of events as accurate as possible when giving my statement after being traumatised and then spending hours being redirected from my GP to the hospital to the police, told to go away and think about it and then finally giving my statement. So that is the best I could recall it, over three years ago. And I'm now trying to recall the same specific details.

Again, what a shame the detective wasn't called as a witness to give his perspective on my presentation when writing my statement.

The defence continued picking apart my statement and order of events suggesting I remembered better now than I did when I wrote it three years ago. I was continually defending myself and clarifying what I did remember.

Still not a peep from the crown prosecutor – (cue cricket sound effect)

I clarified that I did consent to the very first and very normal sexual encounter on the balcony. After yet another untrue suggestion this time regarding the testing in the bathroom. I stated that I pushed his hands off my throat then he swung his arm back to strike me, I blocked the swing, as it came towards me, and I said no.

I had to continue to clarify my order of events and could see how my statement was confusing on this issue. And after not remembering exactly how many trips were made to the bathroom to smoke cannabis the defence suggested I changed my story to which I stated that I didn't have consensual sex after being threatened.

I was fighting in that witness box; I was fighting like I had never fought. I was fighting to be heard with zero legal support. I was divulging all these intimate and horrific sexual details in front of

Trial Day Two: Morning Session

approximately twenty strangers. Trying to concentrate on the defence barrister's questions and every time I looked at her, I see the offender right behind her head.

Still no objections or request for a break from the crown, it was the judge who interrupted the defence during her cross examination and asked me directly, if I would like to take a ten-minute break. Between sobs I replied, yes please.

10:52 a.m. – Cross examination from the defence continues, she outlines that she has an obligation to put forward a certain number of suggestions of what occurred for me to agree or disagree with.

She suggested that the perpetrator didn't ever kneel on my chest the way I described it, to force me to perform oral sex on him.

I replied that is a complete and utter lie.

She suggested that I remembered that incorrectly and that I did indeed perform oral sex on him, but he was lying on his back.

I responded No. No. I did not.

She suggested that he did not ever, using the expression fist me or try to fist me.

To which I replied yes, he did, I do not agree with that.

She suggested that I remembered those details incorrectly and that there was some digital penetration, that is fingers into the vagina but not fisting, as you described.

I replied stating I disagreed.

The defence stated that they understood fisting to be a balled fist inserted into a vagina.

I stated that I didn't think any woman would be able to accommodate a man's fist balled up straight into their vagina, I demonstrated with my own hands the twisting motion that he used to push on my cervix, while he was trying to get his fist in.

Still no peep from the crown prosecutor- (cue crickets) Still no objections.

The defence continued and said again that she was suggesting that there was digital penetration of the vagina, in the order of like one or two fingers, 'if I can call it normal digital penetration of the vagina, but not fisting as you have described it.'

I firmly stated that I believe it was indeed fisting, or an attempt at it and that I had never experienced anything like that in my life.

She suggested that there was absolutely no violence at all, no slapping, no strangulation, no choke hold, no elbows in the chest, no smooshing my face, that it simply didn't happen.

I told the court that I did not agree with that suggestion at all and that was not what happened.

The defence also suggested that the incident referred to as the testing in the bathroom simply never happened either. To which I replied no I did not agree with her suggestion.

Trial Day Two: Morning Session

That he never told me that I couldn't leave, he didn't threaten me to stay, that I never actually said no during the acts, that I didn't ever ask him to stop, that I never mentioned to him in-between the acts that I wasn't into it or that it hurt.

I reminded the defence that yes, those suggestions were true because I had a plan, a plan to survive, no I didn't verbally say no. I told the court with my professional experience my understanding is that women who fight, end up dead. I didn't fight. I didn't say no. I was too frightened.

She also suggested that the perpetrator never said things like, I make the rules and fucking take it. He simply never said that.

I responded with yes, he did, yes he did.

It just went on and on and on.

She said, No saying no? Stop? No punching him? No kicking him? No pushing him off? You did and said nothing to demonstrate to him that you weren't consenting. No swearing at him? No screaming? How far is the police station? It's close by?

I confirmed what she was saying was indeed true, I told the court how I was convincing myself that it was not as bad as it was. Which was a coping mechanism for sure. Because the reality is, that it was as horrific as it was. I wouldn't be disclosing all these intimate details in front of strangers and my family if it didn't happen.

She reminded me that I had access to my mobile phone and could have called or texted whoever I wanted.

Don't Report Rape

And then we are back to the fisting again... Asking me to describe how this occurred, more hand demonstrations.

Still no objection, still silence from the crown.

The judge again, seeing me in distress asks me directly if I would like another break.

I reply to the judge that I really didn't want to, I just wanted it over with. Pleading, I said, I am sure I have answered this question multiple times.

There was some non-verbal communication between the judge and the defence with the judge indicating to the defence prosecutor to move on.

The defence moved on from the fisting to the stretching incident. Again more lovely hand actions demonstrating how the offender stretched my vagina by pulling it apart. Asking me to clarify the order of events. I state that I am honestly not sure of the exact order of things and say in frustration I don't even know how I am expected to know this.

I really don't know; I mean the order of things (mumbling in frustration) I don't know how I am expected to remember the exact order of things.

I state that all I know is that he put his hands in there and tried to ...... fuck *(expression of frustration, yep I swore in court)*....... through sobbing and hyperventilating I apologised to the judge for swearing in the courtroom.

Yep she broke me, cross examination finished at 11:25 a.m.

Trial Day Two: Morning Session

Re-examination by the crown was just a few minutes where she asked me to clarify why I didn't use my phone and why I never left the apartment.

I again went on to explain how I was petrified, I was scared. I was frozen, I even came out of my body for a period of time, which can happen with trauma. Like, I was looking down on my body. With my work in social work, I know that most woman that fight end up dead, so there was no way that I was going to fight. There was no way I was going to scream, there was no way I was going to run. I just had to ride it out, I just had to ride it out.

The crown asked me for further clarity on what I meant by freezing.

I explained it like you are unable to move, you can't, that I would try to tell myself just get up. Just get up! And I – I couldn't.

End of cross re-examination.

That's it, my part was done. My opportunity to speak my truth was over, just like that.

I was excused by the judge and Lesley and I left the courtroom.

I was questioned by the crown, for one hour and I was cross examined by the defence for a total of three hours. That is four hours in total on the stand. Lesley and I followed the crown prosecutor to her office where she consoled me.

I was sobbing and saying things like, 'how, how can she ask things like that?'

Don't Report Rape

The crown prosecutor told me to my face in a very matter of fact way, it was slut shaming, that is what it is, slut shaming, she also told me that I was lucky I didn't get the previous barrister that was allocated this case as he would have absolutely shredded me way more than this barrister did.

Chapter 14

Trial Day Two: Afternoon Session

Next witness called was my good friend Kate who did an amazing job despite several objections from the defence barrister. Kate's recall of events was indeed the same as I had articulated. After just fifteen minutes in the witness box, Kate was excused. Kate was devastated, she felt she had so much more to contribute but unfortunately never had the opportunity.

12:16 p.m. Emergency room doctor examined by the crown. (15 minutes)

Next Witness was the Emergency room doctor who conducted my medical examination, Dr Neil. Dr Neil confirmed his role as a senior medical officer at the local hospital and the most senior doctor available when I presented. Dr Neil provided a brief summary of his qualifications and career. Dr Neil told the same story as both myself and Kate, that is, I had met somebody for a consensual arrangement which started off that way and turned violent during the evening. Dr Neil went through his examination noting my high levels of emotional distress and the physical injuries that he observed and documented. Basically, confirming the bruising on my neck, chest, collar bone, breast, and the backs of my legs. He also confirmed the injuries did not present as old injuries but indeed recent, which again matches with my version of events. Dr Neil confirmed that no internal examination was conducted, and that the genital area was only observed externally to which no injuries were visible, and also highlighting that with his vast experience within the field of emergency medicine and general practice, that even cases confirmed as sexual assault don't always show bruising in the genital area. He confirmed my injuries were indeed consistent with being strangled and kneeled on.

12:24 Cross Examination of Dr Neil by the defence was 30 minutes.

The defence wanted to clarify that despite me telling the doctor I was strangled, and the injuries matched that of being strangled that none of that actually demonstrates to you that somebody was actually strangled. Despite the defence implying that an internal examination was not conducted because there was no evidence suggesting this, Dr Neil explained protocol around examining sexual assault victims and trying to reduce any further trauma. He explained that he would have conducted an internal if there was active bleeding however as there wasn't he didn't want to put me through any further trauma. The defence went on trying to discredit my story and suggest my injuries could have been caused by several different things.

Trial Day Two: Afternoon Session

1:05 p.m. Re-examination of Dr Neil by the crown. (2 minutes)

The crown prosecutor had Dr Neil clarify that everyone bruises differently and that despite the application of force applied to someone's skin, bruising doesn't always show up.

1:07 p.m. Dr Neil was thanked for giving evidence and was excused.

Dr Neil, thank you for your professionalism, respect, and empathy you showed me when presenting that awful day back in Jan 2018. Thank you for your honest recall of events, the documented evidence you provided and most of all… thank you for believing me.

During the break the defence requested the judge speak to the public gallery and remind them that they are to refrain from displaying any signs of distress and must remain silent. The judge addressed the public gallery (which was filled with my family and friends) acknowledging that this is a very delicate and sensitive issue and that it is imperative that the jury remain impartial and not be influenced by anyone in the public gallery. Basically, he told them that they must remain completely emotionless and silent and if they don't it would very well cause a mistrial and we would have to start over again, which would also mean I would need to give evidence again.

2:34 p.m. Jury returned

2:36 p.m. Next witness is Dr Maddry – Forensic Medical Officer examined by the crown (10 minutes).

Dr Maddry stated that he has been a doctor for thirty-six years. The first eight years of his career in hospital practice, the next eight years in general practice and for the past twenty years a forensic medical officer. Dr Maddry was asked to give his opinion in relation to the impacts cannabis and alcohol has on a person's capacity to remember things. Dr Maddry stated that based on my statement and the amount of alcohol and cannabis consumed that it was fair to say I was acutely intoxicated with alcohol and cannabis. Dr Maddry explained how this level of intoxication would cause fragmented memory loss, which means that a person remembers bits and pieces of the night and maybe not in any particular order.

2:47 Cross Examination of Dr Maddry by defence barrister (18 minutes).

Dr Maddry confirmed that in his opinion, I experienced both fragmented and block memory loss. The defence highlighted that people who experience fragmented memory loss continue to interact with others and may engage in potentially dangerous or risky activities that perhaps they normally wouldn't. That while you have the capacity to make decisions while intoxicated, they may not be the same you would make if you weren't intoxicated. It's all part of the reduction of inhibition, increased risk-taking behaviour and poor judgment.

3:04 p.m. – No re-examination by the crown.

3:05 p.m. – Witness excused.

3:05 p.m. – The crown advised the judge that Dr Maddry was the crown's final witness……. Huh? What? How about the detective from QPS? He has been sitting outside the courtroom for the past few days waiting to give evidence. How come the crown decided not to call him. From approximately midday, the defence prosecutor was advising the detective that he would not be required and that

Trial Day Two: Afternoon Session

it wasn't necessary for him to wait around. Despite being told this by the defence, the detective remained in the courthouse. After it was all over, I spoke with the detective about this who stated that he was completely shocked that he was not called as a witness and that in his entire career of policing, he has never <u>not been called</u> as a witness for a sex crime. It appeared that the defence barrister, wasn't feeling well and wanted to wrap things up today so she could return home to Brisbane. So just so we are all on the same page. The detective who arrived at the base hospital, who typed out my statement and who is highly experienced in these types of crimes was NOT called to give evidence. To this day I am still unsure why this decision was made. Perhaps this occurred because of the vast difference in experience between the crown and the defence perhaps the crown was steamrolled by the more mature and experienced defence barrister, I really don't know, and I am not sure I will ever know. Surely, it's standard practice for the investigating officer to give evidence for these types of crimes. Surely, we don't require a law to state this?... as it turns out, maybe we do.

Recommendation 12 – QPS detective must appear as a witness in the trial

Someone from QPS, ideally the investigating officer must give evidence for sexually violent crimes. This must be mandatory and not something prosecutors can opt out of.

The jury retired for a short break while the defence was deciding if the perpetrator was going to give evidence or not. He is not required to but can if he chooses. The perpetrator did decide to give evidence.

3:28 p.m. The perpetrator took the stand and was examined by his barrister (40 minutes).

Her questioning went through how we met and his version of events that evening. So far, his story is matching mine, all up until the first consensual sexual encounter. He stated quite clearly that we absolutely did not have sex on the balcony, he would never do that and in fact suggested we turn down the music out of respect for the neighbours. Such a thoughtful and respectful person, right? Please….. what a load of shit.

Apparently according to the perpetrator, after our first sexual encounter our conversation got kinky and we asked each other about when we last had sex. Here is the rehearsed bit…. Ready….. 'I asked her when she last had anal, as a way for me to know if that would be something she was up for.' Ah so this is his attempt at getting consent according to the current law, the classic - mistake of fact defence.

He went on to describe the oral incident, not surprisingly it was not the same as my version. He claimed …. I was sitting on the edge of the bed, and he was standing. When asked about the kneeling on my chest and pinning my shoulders, he simply said it never happened. Basically, he denied everything; the testing in the bathroom when I blocked his strike, any type of strangulation, hitting, suffocating, choke hold… none if it happened and I simply made it all up. He stated that we had sex approximately eight times over the evening and stated that he even changed condoms when going from anal to vaginal. What a good guy right, how thoughtful. He did confirm that there was no conversation between us about us having anal sex and that it was simply when I had last done it. He claimed that at about 11 p.m. after having sex eight times, we went to sleep and never had sex again. When asked was there

Trial Day Two: Afternoon Session

any kind of rough sex or sex that would include even low levels of violence, he replied no. When asked if that was something he was in to, he stated that he has engaged in rough sex in the past it was not something he would do on a first date with someone he just met.

4:08 p.m. Cross Examination by the crown (12 minutes).

During cross examination the perpetrator confirmed that yes rough sex was something he was in to, yet when asked if he has ever slapped someone during sex, he said no. When asked to define rough sex, he stated that it meant firm and fast, deeper and faster is what he considers rough sex.

Re-examination from the defence (2 minutes).

The defence requested permission from the judge to fat shame me, which she was granted. She asked him about his build at the time, which he stated was similar to his build now. She then asked the offender, after seeing me in court, to comment on my build... yep, read that again. To which he replied that I may have put on a little bit of weight since he saw me last, but not too different. The judge asked the crown if she had any questions with regards to this, she replied no. What a shame the pictures I included with my victim impact statement weren't submitted as they clearly show me at the time of the assault being 20 kg lighter. The defence and the crown were both given my victim impact statement on day one, which included photos of my build, what a shame the jury wasn't shown those images, which would have strengthened my credibility as an honest witness.

4:21 p.m. The perpetrator was stood down.

4:25 p.m. Matter was adjourned for the day.

Wednesday 23rd March

My Tribe update- I went back on the stand today, ripped to shreds from the defence, felt like I was the one on trial.

Next Kate gave her witness statement which was amazing. Then the Dr from the hospital who conducted my medical assessment gave his evidence. Another Dr with expertise in the effects of alcohol and cannabis on memory was next to give evidence. The offender took the stand. End of day. Tomorrow both sides present their closing summaries starting at 9.30. Then the jury deliberates.

I feel today went really well and I am feeling positive for the verdict tomorrow

Chapter 15

Trial Day Three

The jurors are given a list of directs they must consider when deliberating. These instructions are written by the Judge and agreed to by both the crown and the defence.

10:00 a.m. - The defence addresses the jury with her closing argument for the defence (90 minutes).

The main argument was that the events I described just didn't happen. I am having a really hard time reading through this and trying to articulate it to you clearly. She tries to explain to the jury why she felt it necessary to slut shame me and why my sexual experiences with other people before/after the assault is relevant to this case. The defence barrister basically tells the jury that my behaviour after the assault is not consistent of someone who was violently raped and assaulted. What a shame the jury wasn't educated on how people respond to trauma from an actual expert in that field. Furthermore, what a shame the jury didn't get the opportunity to hear from the detective who quite possibly would be considered an expert, having interviewed hundreds of sexual assault victims in his time and would no doubt highlight the vast range of normal responses to crimes of this nature. She reminded the jury to ignore how I presented on the stand, being upset, 'crying and all that,' in her words their decision is purely based on the evidence and not my performance.

She implied that I tended to become more emotional when questioned on particular issues that weren't adding up or when I chopped and changed my answers. She highlighted that I was not afraid to answer her questions because I was so determined to get my point across that I either talked over the top of her or didn't actually answer the question because I was too busy falling over myself, trying to explain why a piece of evidence that didn't look good for me could be explained. The defence reminded the jury that the fact that my memory recall from an event over three years ago is irrelevant and does not mean they should lower their standard of proof. She also told them that it didn't really matter if they thought I was an honest witness, but I had to be an accurate and reliable witness. She also suggested to the jury that the crown will raise the trauma excuse as to why I didn't leave or fight. Again, what a shame the jury didn't hear from an expert in this area, that would indeed explain the trauma response and an automated and unconscious response, well researched, well documented, and certainly not an excuse. The argument focused on my reliability due to intoxication and my trauma response, the fact that I didn't leave or fight.

She told the jury that the reason I was able to give a graphic and detailed description of what occurred was not because it actually

Trial Day Three

did occur but because of my profession as a social worker. She suggested that I may have heard these horrific details from a client or after reading a book and that was how I was able to articulate such horrific details. So now, I guess there is a thing called career shaming, just add that to slut shaming, fat shaming and victim blaming. She also told the jury that the fact that I told the doctor and my friend Kate the same thing does not increase my credibility or make my case any stronger. She said that I was just able to keep the same lie going with everyone that I spoke to about it. The defence also thought it necessary to remind the jury that you don't convict someone of rape because that is all you are hearing in the mainstream media about women speaking up against violence and that this was not an opportunity to cast, effectively, a social vote to speak up for that hashtag Me-Too movement or to wave a flag, you know, at the expense of this man, that is on these serious charges.

The defence finished at 11:37 a.m. court adjourned until after lunch.

12:04 p.m. The crown addresses the jury with her closing argument (34 minutes)

The crown prosecutor's closing argument was brilliant! That little pocket rocket from day one was on fire. Her opening line was a direct quote from me, 'I went there for casual sex, I didn't go there to be strangled, hit and suffocated'.

She went through a number of reasons why the jury should in fact take me as an honest and reliable witness. She reminded the jury that not only should they have been listening to what I had to say but also how I said it and my body language. She suggested that I displayed a natural progression of emotions when talking about the incident. That my so called 'performance' was natural and non-robotic and very much what you would expect from an honest witness recounting an extremely traumatic event. Stating I wasn't putting on crocodile tears and showing you, ladies and gentlemen, that I was putting on a performance. That I wasn't in court trying to sink in the boot, carrying on and making myself look like a victim. I was in fact trying to tell the truth about what happened to me and had no motive to lie. Highlighting I was consistent with the core details, my account of events was logical and rich in detail that only an honest witness can convey.

She told the jury there was no evidence that my injuries could have been caused by someone else. That the strange and specific details I was able to recall would not be possible if it was not true, that what I recalled were indeed real memories, real things that happened to me, real things I remembered. She reminded the jury that compliance or submission to a sexual act is not consent, that consent must be communicated and must be given freely. Also stating the obvious that just because someone has participated in a particular sexual act in the past does not mean she has consented to it in this moment with this person. Again, reminding them that submission was not consent. She highlighted the evidence from Dr Maddry and Kate, how it matched with my version of events and how the jury can use this evidence to help assess my credibility. She mentioned the medical evidence of not only my physical injuries that were examined and documented but also my demeanour and how I presented at the hospital. Injuries identified were bruising to the right side of the neck, bruising to the collar bone, bruising to upper to mid breast region and multiple bruising to the thighs. The doctor explained that the bruising was not old or discoloured but indeed recent. That the shape of the bruising was circular and seemed to resemble finger pressure bruising. She finished by saying that my evidence was detailed, clear and did not present

Trial Day Three

as lies but as an honest and reliable witness and as such should convict him on all charges.

Court retired for lunch and resumed at 1:45 p.m.

The judge went through with the jury and summarised the case and explained how the law applies to each situation. He explained that each charge must be looked at and assessed individually, however it was an all or nothing case, all guilty or all not guilty, either they believed me or they didn't. Hang on, what happened to 'we just need one guilty? All or nothing… how can this be? The judge explained that the issue of consent was the main matter.

Two elements the jury must be satisfied with, beyond a reasonable doubt are.

1. That the defendant did assault me.
   Meaning any person who strikes, touches, or moves or otherwise applies force of any kind to the person directly or indirectly without the person's consent.

2. That the assault was unlawful.
   That is, it was not justified, authorised or excused by the law.

The judge explained that if the jury was satisfied with both of those elements, they would return a guilty verdict on all charges. If they were not satisfied with those two elements, beyond a reasonable doubt, they would return a not guilty verdict on all charges. This case was purely based on if the jury believed me or not. The jury must be satisfied beyond a reasonable doubt that I was an honest, credible, and reliable witness. If I was, then it would be a guilty verdict, if they were not satisfied beyond a reasonable doubt that I was an honest witness then it would be a not guilty verdict.

However, then the jury must take into account the law regarding the mistake of fact defence.

A lot of the instructions to the jury included details on the mistake of fact defence. The judge explained that the law provides that a person who commits an act under the honest and reasonable belief, even though mistaken belief, is not criminally responsible for the act. So even if the jury did believe me, my version of events and believed I did not consent, so long as they believed that the perpetrator honestly and reasonably believed I did consent, then it's not a crime. It's a get out of jail free card used by sex offenders, *oops sorry I thought you were into it!* This has been a documented loophole in our justice system for decades.

Amy MacMahon – Greens MP for South Brisbane put forward a bill to amend consent laws to remove the mistake of fact defence and introduce an affirmative consent model. Unfortunately, twelve months before my trial the labour government did not support this bill and voted down her amendments. Here is what she had to say about it on social media.

Amy MacMahon – Greens MP for South Brisbane

BREAKING: Labor has just voted down my amendments to introduce an affirmative model of consent in Queensland laws. Before you scroll on, I want to explain how this will perpetuate rape culture and make it easier for rapists to beat charges.

I can't describe how disappointing, and at points absolutely harrowing, it's been in parliament this week. I've watched as

Trial Day Three

Labor and LNP members, one after the other, stood up and said how important it is to believe women, how they stand with them.

But they won't stand with the victim survivors that have come forward with their stories of how the Queensland legal system has failed them.

And they won't stand with the dozen frontline organisations that sent an open letter to Premier Annastacia Palaszczuk and Attorney-General Shannon Fentiman, calling on them to amend their Consent (Mistake of Fact) Bill to include an affirmative consent model.

Perhaps even more harrowing than their hypocrisy on such an important issue, is how it's felt like they are gaslighting us. Yesterday I heard the Attorney General herself describe how 'silence does not amount to consent' in law in Queensland.

This is a blatant oversimplification, and one with grave consequences for victims and survivors of sexual assault.

Under the current law – which is reflected in Labor's Bill that passed unamended today – consent cannot be inferred from silence or a lack of resistance, for example if they freeze, or are intoxicated, asleep or unconscious. But defendants CAN (and do) still use these factors to beat charges, by arguing they had a 'mistaken belief' that the other person consented.

Too many of us know someone with a story like this – where a person goes to someone's house, expresses an interest in having sex, then falls asleep only to wake up to the other person raping them. It is an absolute failure of our laws, and of this Government, that the other person could beat rape charges in that case using the 'mistaken belief' defence.

Don't Report Rape

This is why I moved amendments to:

- Introduce an affirmative definition of consent
- Require the defendant to show they took positive and reasonable steps to ascertain the other person's consent if they're arguing a 'mistaken belief' in consent
- Remove the ability to argue a mistaken belief in consent where the claimant was unconscious, asleep, or intoxicated and had not positively expressed consent.

Bizarrely, Labor MPs repeatedly stood up and said today that they knew advocates and survivors weren't happy with the Bill. Their answer is to re-do consultation, asking them to tell their stories and give their feedback on the same issue again, after they've just been blatantly ignored.

No one is pretending that laws alone will end sexual violence – that requires broad-scale, systemic and social education and change. BUT our laws should reflect the society we want to live in, and right now Queensland Labor is saying that affirmative consent isn't important.

It's cowardly, it's shameful, and it's potentially re-traumatising for victims and survivors.

To everyone who's experienced rape or sexual assault only to have a defendant claim they 'thought it was OK' because of outdated rape myths, I am so sorry. I'm furious.

And I will not stop fighting.

Amy MacMahon – Greens MP for South Brisbane

Trial Day Three

3 Reasons
Why the bill to amend the criminal code (sexual consent laws) has been described as a slap in the face to survivors:

1. It still allows defendants to beat rape charges by arguing they believed their victim/survivor consented – even if they didn't ask (often called the 'mistake of fact defence').
2. Defendants can still use the mistake of fact loophole even if the person was asleep, unconscious or heavily intoxicated
3. The onus is still on victim survivors to communicate their lack of consent.

I'm calling on the Queensland Government to listen to sexual assault survivors and legislate affirmative consent now.

Survivors of sexual assault and advocates have been calling for an affirmative model of consent. The consent law reform bill that Qld Labor is pushing through parliament this week has ignored these calls.

Here's a quick explainer on what's happening

What is affirmative consent?

Essentially, affirmative consent requires a positive, clear and freely given 'yes'. Consent needs to be given for different acts within a sexual encounter, and for the people involved, steps have been taken to actively ascertain consent, and requires a person demonstrates an ongoing willingness to engage in a sexual act either verbally or through their actions.

Active agreement cannot be implied. It must be clearly and positively expressed.

For me, this kind of model acknowledges that it requires an ongoing conversation between the people involved, and the responsibility the person initiating sex, or something new within sex, to find out whether the other person consents, and continues to consent.

In what way does Qld Labor's consent law reform bill not include an affirmative model of consent?

The minor changes in this bill still mean that the onus is on victim survivors to express non-consent or actively resist. In an affirmative model of consent, the onus is on the party initiating an act to obtain consent from the other person.

The bill also does not mandate the need for the party initiating an act to take active steps to seek consent.

Attorney-General Shannon Fentiman has even acknowledged that this bill doesn't legislate an affirmative consent model.

An article in News.com.au articulated Ms MacMahon's last ditched efforts to get her bill passed. Written by James P Hall.

A last-ditch effort to modify Queensland's new consent laws before they passed through Parliament has been shot down.

Greens MP Amy McMahon, spurred on by advocates who believe the laws fail to protect women, made a last-ditch attempt to add an affirmative consent model to the bill, which proposed the need to require clear and more enthusiastic agreement before taking part in a sexual act.

But this was voted down by both the government and the opposition, with Ms McMahon taking to social media, vowing to, 'not stop fighting'.

Trial Day Three

'I'm furious,' the member for South Brisbane tweeted after her amendments were rejected.

'To everyone who's experienced rape or sexual assault, only to have a defendant claim they 'thought it was OK' because of outdated rape myths, I am so sorry.'

The affirmative consent amendments were backed by women's rights and rape advocates who say the reforms passed on Thursday fail to adequately protect victims of sexual assault.

'It's following on from a Queensland Law Reform Commission report that failed to listen to survivors, failed to listen to rape and women advocates and pretty much only listened to the lawyers,' Women's Legal Service chief executive Angela Lynch told reporters on Wednesday.

'The laws and the system is weighted in favour of the perpetrator.'

The leading women's rights advocate said a common response for a rape victim was to freeze during the attack, which she says could be interpreted as consent under the new law.

'You can't assume that somebody who is frozen, someone who is unconscious, someone who just hasn't said anything is enough,' she said.

'The woman doesn't believe she has consented; she's actually frightened but often it can be argued in court to take it (the complaint) further.'

Ms Lynch said the 'figures speak for themselves'.

'Possibly between 20,000 and 40,000 rapes occur in Queensland each year, around 6500 charges go to the police, and we have just around 300 convictions,' she said.

'Many victims do not come forward because of the trauma of the criminal justice system itself.'

The Attorney-General said the amendments were an 'important step to modernise consent laws' but admitted more could be done.

She said the Palaszczuk government was open to amending the bill once it was passed but rejected the assertion a frozen or silent victim could be viewed as providing consent, insisting the 'law is making it clear that silence is not consent'.

'I understand that some stakeholders believe that our laws could have gone further, and our government is absolutely committed to looking at anything we can do to keep women safe and hold perpetrators to account,' Ms Fentiman said.

Thank you, Amy MacMahon, for your continued fight on this issue, we will keep fighting they can't ignore the masses. The reality is that if Ms MacMahon's bill was passed, my perpetrator would be in jail.

Recommendation 13 – Amend consent laws to an affirmative model

Consent laws must be amended to an affirmative consent model to remove the mistake of fact defence, the commonly known loophole that allows rapists to walk free.

Trial Day Three

The judge continued with his summary of the case to the jurors taking approximately three hours to do so.

2:43 p.m.- The jury was retired to consider their verdict.

I nervously waited with my friends and family to hear if they have reached a verdict. After just thirty minutes we were advised that the jury had reached their verdict. My partner Jamie had ducked out to pick up kids and we truly thought it would take longer to deliberate. Unfortunately, I did not have him for support when the verdict was read but I did have my tribe of family and friends in the courtroom. I entered the courtroom and sat next to Lesley and my sister, holding each of their hands. While waiting for the trial to resume in the courtroom we sat and watched the crown prosecutor and the defence barrister have a friendly discussion about menopause and hot flashes, laughing with each other over general chit chat before court resumed. The defence barrister had already changed into her casual wear so I assumed she was going straight to the airport to catch her flight home. Remember if the detective was called as a witness the trial would have dragged into the next day. This all seemed extremely unprofessional and certainly not something one would see in a Brisbane courtroom, but who knows, may very well be standard practice.

Chapter 16

The Verdict

The jury entered the courtroom in a single file and they stood in silence as the nominated speaker, a tall man with a ginger beard read out the verdict on each charge, one by one. On the count of blah blah blah… We the jury ... blah blah blah finds the defendant... Not guilty. No one could believe what we were hearing, I fell into Lesley's chest and just sobbed and sobbed. The courtroom became a little chaotic, the judge and jury left the court room.

The perpetrator threw his hands up in celebration yelling 'I'm innocent', I lunged forward held back by Lesley and my sister and said to him directly,

'Look me in the eyes and tell me your innocent,' he wouldn't even look at me.

Don't Report Rape

Despite being cleared of all charges and free to leave the courtroom the perpetrator sat next to the security guard and waited for us to leave. After we left the local paper reported hearing him sobbing in the dock.

We didn't know what to do, thankfully right at this time my good friend Cristel arrived, entered the courtroom and ushered us out and we all headed to my home where Jamie met us. I was absolutely distraught and devastated. Unable to talk, uncontrollably sobbing and I just remember that I kept saying, 'I don't understand. I don't understand.'

I ended up taking a sedative and wondered why the fuck I even tried to hold a violent sex offender accountable, what was the point and that it was all for nothing.

24th March

My tribe update – NOT GUILTY on all seven counts, absolutely devastating

27th March

My Tribe update – received this from a dear friend, amazing human and fellow sister Sasha Marie Tagg on the day the 'not guilty' verdict was read. I have only been able to open it today. Jamie and I sobbed through the entire song. It touched my heart so deeply.

The Verdict

Shared with permission

Trish, I don't have words... when I don't have words I turn to music. Then the words flow. I want to do something for you. I stand with you, I believe you, every single word. You have stood up, and by doing this, you have advocated for so many other people, the voices they could not use, to end sexual violence. I know it's incredibly hard right now, I am looking up to you like a warrior woman and nothing will stop this feeling. I thank you for being courageous enough to speak out about this unforgivable behaviour. Your strength is undeniable. I am here for you.

Written, played, and sung beautifully by Sasha Tagg. To hear this song, please head to my website https://www.trishwyatt.com.au

Don't Report Rape

Lyrics

Shatter my body

Play with my life

Walking to nowhere

Twist the knife

I only want to stand next to you,

Lift your head when it's got a frown

Be your feet when you cannot walk

Treading water so you won't drown

We've got you sister

The pieces it'll take time,

To heal and feel well,

What you've done for the voiceless,

So endless to tell

For our daughters and sons,

teach right and watch them and grow

Timing means nothing just speak up,

No means no

NO MEANS NO

No matter how you feel it's real to just give up,

such a space and time you just want to throw up,

fuck the justice system I think I just threw up,

The Verdict

to let a man walk free and rape a body up... when its owner said no, what a pitiful show, let the feelings flow, but do not let them take control...

Remember your Honour, Strength, Resilience

Truth, Voice, Light

Life that you spoke your truth... and we believe and stand by you....

We believe and thank you too...

I only want to stand next to you

Lift your head when you've got a frown

Be your feet when you cannot walk

Treading water so you won't drown

Message from Kate who has been with me since day one – Hi Lovely, I listened to the song on our drive back from Cloncurry whilst watching the outback scenery pass me by out the car window. I did have some tears. It's such a beautiful and powerful song. I'm feeling so many emotions. Relieved that court is over but bitterly disappointed and angered by the outcome and the impact of this injustice on you. The firsthand experience of how heavily weighted the justice system is towards perpetrators is one I won't forget. I am OK though and I am always here for you Trish xxx.

27th March 2022

My Tribe Update – To say I'm shattered is an understatement. The violent animal who raped and tortured me repeatedly over eight hours in Jan 2018 has been found NOT GUILTY on all seven counts.

Don't Report Rape

The offender's defence was that my whole story was a lie, that we had a lovely night of chatting, laughing and consensual sex. End of story.

Despite photographic evidence of injuries, an emergency department report by a Dr documenting injuries and an admission by the offender that he did not obtain consent.

The offender had his partner and mother present at court. The whole time he was slumped over, head hung and mumbled talking. Along with bouts of sobbing while in his glass box in the court room. He even needed time out to pull himself together from hyperventilating. Yep poor fella.

I was absolutely roasted by the defence on the stand for hours and over two days. Intimate details, gory details I had to describe over and over and over whilst trying to recall an incident that occurred over three years ago. I was absolutely distraught, slut-shamed (that's allowed in court), victim-blamed (why didn't you fight, run, scream etc) unfortunately it was me that was on trial. My only other witness was my friend and ex-colleague Kate who was amazing but was constantly cut off and objected to, she was only on the stand five to 10 mins. I'm sorry for the women who are yet to be assaulted by this animal in the future, because there will be, just like there were victims before me, this is what he does. Our community is not safe, and he should be in jail.

Key failures
What is a trauma response?

There was no trauma expert called to explain to the jury the flight, fight, freeze and fawn response. A heavily researched, debated and peer reviewed issue, common knowledge these days. Any

The Verdict

doctor, psychologist, psychiatrist, nurse, social worker, or counsellor would be able to explain and discuss this. It explains how our body responds under horrific fear, particularly life-threatening fear. It explains why victims of rape don't run, scream, or fight. Statistically the most common response is freeze and fawn, and in fact, those who have fought end up dead.

Lead Detective- After hanging around the court for three days waiting to be called to give evidence, the Snr Detective was advised by the defendant's lawyer that he was not required. The QPS Senior Detective involved with my case from the moment I reported, the officer who took my statement.....was NOT called to give evidence. Crown prosecutor told me she didn't think he had anything to offer.....

The offender didn't do himself any justice when he took the stand which was only for about 20 mins, answering with yes, no responses. The crown's closing argument was good and strong, it counter attacked everything the defence argued. We were feeling strong. Confident on at least three out of the seven. Absolutely shocked by the verdict after only 30 mins deliberating, I'm still coming to terms with it.

Once the offender was free to go, he didn't even have the guts to walk past us. He did throw his arms up celebrating his innocence but refused to look me in the eye.

We were so shell shocked, thankfully my amazing friend Cristel arrived at the courthouse with perfect timing as mum was about to faint, Cristel grabbed mum while my sister got her a chair, then scooped me up and instructed everyone to leave, we headed home.

Recommendation 14 – Psychological support for victims

Victims of violent sexual crimes must have a professional support person they can access during the trial. This is in addition to the victim's legal representative; this is someone experienced in trauma who is able to provide emotional support for victim and their family during the trial and leading up to the trial.

Where to now everyone says?

Well, there are currently ninety women waiting for a trial for violent sexual crimes made against them here in my regional community, that is what the crown prosecutor told me. Yes, ninety and my advice to them is... withdraw, pull out, don't go to trial and don't report rape to police.

I am disgusted and appalled at the system, we need to refuse to participate in it until it's overhauled. Yes, more women are going to be assaulted but until it's some big wigs daughter, granddaughter, sister or friend, nothing is going to change. This fight has been going on for decades, enough is enough.

Everyone in the court room knew he did it, what possible motive would I have to make this up. I have PTSD as a direct result of the assault, I lost my career as a social worker due to the PTSD, I am on a disability pension because of the assault. But no, we weren't allowed to mention this, not relevant. However, it all comes down to a technical issue in the way the consent laws are written.

The Verdict

Special thanks to everyone who has been supporting me, you have no idea how your words of support gave me strength, even in my darkest days.

My amazing family, I am so grateful for my family, they have stood by me and helped me in so many ways over the past three years. This has taken a huge toll on them too.

My beautiful Jamie, I truly don't think I'd be alive today if it wasn't for this amazing human. Your unconditional love, support, understanding, and encouragement is admirable. Forever grateful.

Everyone who attended court, thank you.

Kate who has been with me since day one, who also has had this hanging over her head for over three years to take the stand as a witness.

And the amazing Lesley who supported me while I gave evidence in the closed court room and a pillar of strength for me during the trial.

DON'T REPORT RAPE, not yet anyway, not until they change things.

Unfortunately, as the verdict was not guilty, I never had the opportunity to read the victim impact statement I wrote. So here it is, this is what I would have read out in the courtroom, had he been found guilty and convicted.

Victim Impact Statement

The crimes committed by the offender of which he has been found guilty have had a devastating impact, not only in my life but also my family including my parents, siblings and my four children. Six months before the assault I left my 20-year marriage and was the primary carer of my four children who were aged one, five, ten and twelve. The assault occurred on the last weekend before I was due to return from maternity leave to my job as a full-time social worker. My role was in Intensive Family Support, working with families experiencing abuse and neglect.

Career and financial Impact

I attempted to return to my job many times with flexible and reduced hours, my role involved going into family's homes where abuse a neglect were occurring and work intensively with the family to reduce the harm to the children. I was extremely passionate about this work as it is much needed in our community, and I felt like I was making a difference. However, since the assault, I never felt safe enough to conduct a home visit. I experienced several triggers related to the assault including every time I put a car seatbelt on, as the pressure on my neck would trigger intrusive thoughts of being strangled. I also had trouble reading the referrals as they led the family's history of violence and trauma. This again triggered intrusive thoughts and replays of the event in my mind leaving me unable to focus and concentrate. With the support of my employer, I transferred into the Foster Care team and while this role felt safer, I was still unable to remain employed due to the triggers, extreme tiredness, fatigue, lack of concentration, anxiety, irritability and feeling numb. I decided to resign. After a few months of not working, I accepted a full-time job in a youth refuge. The refuge had great security with lots of cameras, I felt much safer however when a young person became aggressive, I froze and was unable to press the distress alarm. This was my last attempt at getting back into the workforce. I no longer feel I can work in the social services industry. This had a cascading effect on my self-esteem, self-worth, and my identity as a whole. Who was I now? I'm not a social worker? Due to the PTSD I suffer, I am now on a disability pension. Going from an $80,000 annual income to a $20,000 annual income has had an extremely devastating impact on my finances and ability to provide basic needs for myself and my four children. This led to further thoughts of hopelessness, depression, and negative thought patterns.

Parenting and impact on my children

Prior to the assault I was a patient, present and engaged mother. After the assault my injuries were so debilitating, I had to have my mother move in and live with me to help me care for myself and my four children. Still needing more support, we had to move houses to be closer to my brother and sister who assisted my mother to care for me and my children. The excessive sleeping, inability to get out of bed and emotional numbness prevented me from being the patient, present and engaged mother I used to be. I was now asleep a lot of the time, irritable, quick to anger and disconnected emotionally. During my worst days my mum would cook, clean, grocery shop, do the washing, school drop offs and pickups and bath the kids. This burden now falls on my fiancé as my mum no longer lives with me. This causes me to feel a lot of guilt for not being able to do the things I use to. What upsets me the most about this was the impact this had on my youngest as he was only one year old when the assault occurred. My injuries robbed me and my son of our ability to bond, which I will never get back. My mum would often bring my son into my room where I was sleeping and lay him with me just to have that physical closeness even though I was numb and disconnected emotionally. My older two children who are now in high school have difficulty at school during assemblies or class discussions on consent and sexual assault. Along with support from the school, they are both accessing psychologists for support. The parental guilt I feel is overwhelming, my children deserve better, my children deserve the parent I was before.

Social Impact

Prior to the assault I was outgoing and social. Now, I spend most of my time at home as that is where I feel safe and the most comfortable. Being out in the community doesn't feel very safe for me anymore, I even dyed and changed my hair in case I did see the offender hoping he wouldn't recognise me. I have experienced the following triggers; the car seatbelt, as mentioned previously, I generally use my left hand to hold the seatbelt off my neck when I'm in a car to prevent the unwanted distressing memories, people who look similar to the offender, men with neck tattoos and anxiety that I may see the offender in our small community, which includes when I'm driving and approaching road works as I know the offender works on road works. I avoid watching TV shows or movies that involve violence and sexual violence as these trigger unwanted traumatising memories of the assault that replay through my mind like a movie on repeat that I can't stop. I also avoid the location where the assault occurred for the same reasons. These triggers leave me in a state of hyper vigilance, constantly on the lookout for danger and startled by loud noises. If I do go out, I will generally always have someone with me and at any time I can get a sudden urge to go home urgently and if I can't get home quickly it has led to severe anxiety and panic attacks. During mandatory mask wearing, just the thought of having something over my mouth and nose was enough to trigger a panic attack. I had to see my GP and request an exemption letter which I carried on me in case I was forced to put a mask on. In public during this time I experienced horrified looks, shaking heads and comments from our community as to why I should have a mask on and how selfish I was for not wearing one. The impact on my life socially has put a strain on my interpersonal relationships, often I'm not motivated to maintain relationships leaving me feeling detached and isolated. Again, contributing to negative self-worth, self-esteem and guilt for not being the friend I use to be.

Physical impact

Physically I am also very different. I used to take pride in my appearance, I wore makeup and dressed professionally these days I don't wear makeup and I'm not fussed on what I wear. I have gone through several different medications to help address my symptoms trying to find the right fit and as such I have put on over 20 kgs, a common side effect to these types of medications. My sleep has also been affected by the assault as I sleep excessively as a way to cope and escape. I also experience nightmares which involve me calling out for help in my sleep and thrashing or fighting in bed while I am asleep. I then wake up startled, frightened and confused. This impacts my fiancé whose sleep is disrupted as it wakes him up and he spends time calming me down and helping me get back to sleep. I have also experienced heart palpitations, panic attacks, hand tremors, excessive sweating, chills, rashes, and involuntary twitching which increases during times of stress.

Intimacy

When I first met my fiancé I told him straight away about the assault, how it has impacted me and how it may impact our relationship. Not having been with anyone since the assault, I experienced a lot of anxiety as to how it would be, would I be triggered, and could I ever enjoy sexual intimacy again? While my fiancé was extremely patient supportive and understanding I still experience triggers that cause distressing unwanted memories, fear, and panic during sexual intimacy. It may be a simple touch to my neck or face, the heaviness of his body on mine, physical closeness that leaves me feeling suffocated and unable to breathe. Sometimes

I am unable to pinpoint the exact thing that I was triggered by which is frustrating and confusing.

Psychologically

I was formally diagnosed with Major Depression and Post Traumatic Stress Disorder. My treatment team consists of my GP, Psychiatrist and Psychologist. The symptoms of these illnesses range in severity day to day but there have been times when feelings of hopelessness, negative self-talk and disconnection are at its worst is when I experience a heaviness of being so overwhelmed, so deep in a thickness that I can't see a way out. So unwell that simply running away and abandoning my children or taking my own life, seemed the only way out. This is a frightening place to be, not only for me, but also my loved ones supporting me. My families support to keep me alive has been heroic, to this day my Dad who lives in Sydney calls me at 4 p.m. every single day to check in and make sure I am doing OK. I completely understand why victims of rape and sexual assault don't report to police, not only are you trying to process and heal from what happened to you, but you are also waiting for your day in court. I am often caught up in thoughts about the trial, trying to prepare for my reputation and character to be questioned and shredded, my family and friends hearing the horrific and intimate details and the shame and embarrassment attached to this. I am grieving the loss of who I was; the mother, daughter, sister, friend and the professional I was before the assault. She doesn't exist anymore, and she never will. To this day, almost three years since the assault and intense therapy I am still coming to terms with who I am now as opposed to who I was.

This victim impact statement has been extremely confronting and difficult to write. To see the many ways in which my life has been impacted and how different my life is now compared to how it was before causes great sadness.

Chapter 17

Where to from here?

Below is a list of the 14 recommendations for the law makers, recommendation I believe should be implemented immediately, as a matter of urgency.

Recommendation 1 – All trials MUST have a trauma expert as a witness

All sexually violent cases must have a trauma expert as a witness for the trial to educate the jury on trauma responses and stop blaming the victim for how she responded.

Recommendation 2 – Social workers must be available at the emergency department in hospitals for when victims of sexual assault present.

Social workers must be available to hospital emergency departments, when required. This is a highly traumatic experience in a very public environment, someone trained in psychological first aid is vital.

Recommendation 3 – Staff trained to conduct rape kits in hospitals

Multiple staff must be trained to conduct rape kits in regional hospitals and someone qualified must be available every single day. No rape victim should miss out on this vital step.

Recommendation 4 – Legal Representation must be mandatory right from the start

Victims of sexual violence must have their own legal representation who can advise them right from the moment of reporting and through until the trial is completed.

Recommendation 5 – QPS timing of arresting violent sex offenders

   a) Every single officer should know how to appropiatley respond to a person reporting a sex crime.
   b) Timing of arresting violent sex offenders. A review of procedures and policies is required, at least for my local police station, I am unsure how this relates to other police stations in the state. Surely, no one believes a violent rapist should be given free rein in our community for twenty days?
   c) QPS should be maintaining contact and offering updates and support to victims while waiting for trial.

Recommendation 6 – Strangulation must be a stand-alone crime

Strangulation laws that are current under domestic violence laws, need to be included in criminal law. Strangulation is strangulation. Someone puts their hands around your throat, tightens their grip to prevent you from breathing, without consent. It IS A CRIME if you are in a relationship with the offender but NOT A CRIME if it's a stranger?

Recommendation 7 – DPP accountability and wait time for trial

Whilst keeping victims up to date with their case is current policy and stated as such in the 'Charter of Victims Rights', this did not happen for me. I was not advised in November 2018 when the charges were changed, I was advised one year later. Something is wrong with processes or procedures that allowed this to occur. A victim having to wait over 3 years for a trial is unacceptable and needs to be rectified immediately…. This may be more judges, prosecutors, courtrooms, admin staff, monthly sittings for regional communities instead of bimonthly… what ever is required to reduce this time must be done.

Recommendation 8 - Jury Selection procedure updated

Scrap the current program used to select potential jurors for jury duty and implement an up to date, trauma informed program that is able to exclude victims of serious crimes to prevent further trauma.

Recommendation 9 – Laws specific to sexual violence

We need crimes specific to sexual violence, right now our system only takes into account rape, which is penetration without consent. I believe there should also be rape with violence laws to cover these violent acts of sexual violence. There is a big difference from being raped which is horrific enough, let alone being raped and physically assaulted at the same time particularly to the point that you may actually die. Sexual violence as defined by Queensland Government website is 'Sexual Violence (including sexual abuse and assault) is any unwanted sexual behaviour towards another person'. Personally, I don't think this is good enough.

With rough sex becoming more 'normal' as seen in porn, tv shows and movies. It needs to be defined within the law. Rough Sex can be split into two categories. Mild and playful rough sex includes spanking and hair pulling while violent rough sex includes slapping, strangulation, fisting and suffocation. Consent for rough sex must be gained through an affirmative consent model and must include an agreement on a safe word, in which either party can use to stop all interactions immediately.

Recommendation 10 – Ban slut shaming in our courtrooms
No surprise here. It's clearly quite easy for defence prosecutors to obtain permission from a judge to slut shame a victim on the stand during cross examination. The criminal law act (sexual offences) Act clearly needs re-writing. What is the point of having a law to prevent slut shaming and victim blaming if prosecutors can still ask permission to do it under special circumstances?

Recommendation 11 – Trauma informed courtrooms
My local Court was recently renovated surely a more trauma informed configuration of the courtroom could have been taken into account.

Recommendation 12 – QPS detective must appear as a witness in the trial
Someone from QPS, ideally the investigating officer must give evidence for sexually violent crimes. This must be mandatory and not something prosecutors can opt out of.

Recommendation 13 – Amend consent laws to an affirmative model
Consent laws must be amended to an affirmative consent model to remove the mistake of fact defence, the commonly known loophole that allows rapists to walk free.

Where to from here?

Recommendation 14 – Psychological support for victims
Victims of violent sexual crimes must have a professional support person they can access during the trial. This is in addition to the victim's legal representative; this is someone experienced in trauma who is able to provide emotional support for victims and their family during the trial and leading up to the trial.

My Advice to Survivors

Firstly, I am truly sorry this has happened to you. This was not your fault and I believe you.

Build your tribe, create a private group of people who love and support you. They will hold you when you can't stand, and they will encourage you to keep fighting.

Remember you are so much stronger than you think, and nothing can break you. You will grieve the person you were before the assault but the person you become after the assault is the warrior you have always been.

With regards to reporting, by all means, go to your local police station and tell them what happened so there is a record, but DO NOT prosecute, DO NOT try to hold the offender accountable; the way the system is currently, it's just not worth it.

Focus on your healing. Find a psychologist you connect with. Explore the vast array of alternative healing; tapping, journaling, art, sound, drumming, animal therapy, inner child work, somatic body work, massage, meditation, energy healing, get out in the fresh air and most importantly; try to feel everything, feel it, acknowledge it and release it. Numbing feelings or memories

Don't Report Rape

with substance or medication will just delay your healing. While medication is helpful at times and it was for me that is for sure, it's not the long-term answer. No one can heal you from this, except you, and you will get there and once you are there you won't believe how far you have come. Grab your shield, you are a fucking warrior.

Appendix 1

Trauma Response referencing

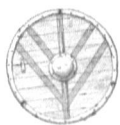

Responses to trauma have been researched and documented for decades by both academics and leaders in the field of psychology and psychiatry.

Global leaders and Experts in the field
Pete Walker, M.A. Psychotherapy
Best-selling Trauma Research Author | Bessel van der Kolk, MD.
Trauma - Dr. Gabor Maté
Stephen W. Porges, PhD | Polyvagal Theory
Dr. Dan Siegel Home Page - Dr. Dan Siegel
Richard Schwartz, PhD — The Trauma Therapist Project

Queensland Government websites and statistics

You will notice our Government articulates the issues of sexual violence well, including the issues of victim blaming and a the many flaws in the judicial system however, significant change is yet to occur.

Recovery from sexual violence | Community support | Queensland Government

Sexual violence prevention | Department of Justice and Attorney-General

Sexual Violence in Queensland - Key Facts - QSAN

About the Author

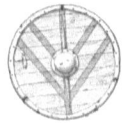

This is the first book by Trish Wyatt which has come to fruition after she survived a horrific life-threatening rape and her fight for justice in what she describes as a barbaric, outdated, and cruel justice system.

Trish grew up in South-West Sydney attending a local catholic high school, she completed grade twelve in 1995. Her passion for social services was sparked after supporting her mother through some serious mental health issues and is when Trish returned to study as a mature age student and went on to obtain a Bachelor of Applied Social Science.

Trish enjoyed a vast career in social services including her first role at The Wayside homeless drop-in centre in Kings Cross Sydney to the rural and remote communities of Roma and surrounds in Queensland. Trish worked with some of our most vulnerable and forgotten members of our community, and she did so with the upmost compassion, empathy, and respect.

Don't Report Rape

Trish has four children and was married for twenty years until she ended her marriage in 2017. Trish now resides in beautiful regional Queensland. Trish with her four children, her fiancé Jamie and his three children call themselves 'perfectly blended'. Trish and Jamie are due to be married in October 2022.

Speaker Bio

Trish Graham is an experienced social worker turned author and activist. She is passionate about raising awareness of sexual violence and our archaic "justice" system where it is almost impossible to convict dangerous sex offenders, and where victims of sexual crimes experience further trauma.

Trish provides a raw and very personal insight into her lived experience after surviving an extremely violent and life-threatening rape and assault in the regional Queensland town of Bundaberg in 2019.

The assault itself was disturbing and shocking, but what followed - from the moment she tried to report the crimes and the more than three years wait for the trial - beggars belief. So horrendous was her post-crime experience, that her genuine advice to survivors is not to report rape.

With the current state of our "justice" system and laws pertaining to sexual violence, Trish shockingly claims that pursuing perpetrators of serious sexual crimes will most likely lead to further anguish for the victim.

In order for change to occur, Trish advocates for updating consent laws, demanding trauma informed practice in the judicial system, and to stop the victim blaming and slut shaming which is currently permitted in our court rooms.

Trish is a courageous survivor of a heinous sexual attack who is determined to be heard, not only through her own story, but also by providing a voice to women and girls who have been a victim of sexual violence and been able to speak. Women who may have never told a soul, women who were unable to report and women who blame themselves and, most importantly, women who have taken their life waiting for trial.

You will be inspired by Trish's bravery and the inner warrior she discovered during this life-altering experience.

Three key issues Trish is passionate about making are:

- Find out first hand what it is like for a survivor to report these types of crimes in Queensland Australia
- Hear how victim blaming and slut shaming currently take place in our courtrooms
- Gain an understanding into the 'Mistake of Fact' defence loophole that allows rapists to walk free and why we only have a 3% conviction rate for rape

Acknowledgements

I would like to acknowledge the amazing love and support I have had from my family, my parents, my sister, her husband, my brother and his wife. My family have been right beside me this whole time, having to hear what I had been through and not being able to do anything about it, experiencing the injustice alongside me. I know how hard this has been on them and I am eternally grateful. My mum who lived with me, took care of me and took care of my children. I would not have made it through without you mum, thank you

My four beautiful children. Not only were they trying to adjust to the divorce of their parents, having to move house four times in three years, new schools etc. but they also witnessed how the assault impacted me, on a daily basis.

My absolutely amazing fiancé Jamie whose love, compassion and optimism helped me through some of my darkest days. A man who put my faith back in love and humanity. A man who makes me laugh, so hard, every single day. A man whose eyes light up every time he sees me. A man I never knew even existed, who I affectionately call 'My Jamie'. I adore you, thank you for being you.

Jamie along with his three children have merged with myself and my four children to create our perfectly blended family. Jamie and I are getting married in October 2022, our home is busy and noisy, but it is full of love and acceptance. I thank each of you for your encouragement and support to tell my story.

I started to write this book three months after the trial finished and it took seven weeks to get my first draft.

Massive thanks and gratitude to the 76 members of my private FB group called 'My Tribe'. I created this group not long after the assault to keep family and friends updated and it turned into a powerful source of support. The members of this group consisted of female friends and family from various areas of my life; childhood, school, university, Sydney, colleagues and neighbours. Thank you, every single one of you, even if you never posted anything, I felt so much love and support. A number of women in this group suggested quite a few times that I should write a book, thank you for your belief in me.

Here it is…. I did it!

www.ingramcontent.com/pod-product-compliance
Lightning Source LLC
Chambersburg PA
CBHW030259100526
44590CB00012B/452